THE MYSTERY OF JOAN OF ARC

LÉON DENIS

Translated by
ARTHUR CONAN DOYLE

CONTENTS

Translator's Preface	1
Introduction	5
1. Domrémy	17
2. The Situation In 1429	22
3. The Infancy Of Joan Of Arc	25
4. Vaucouleurs	32
5. Chinon, Poitiers And Tours	37
6. Orleans	47
7. Reims	52
8. Compiègne	61
9. Rouen—The Prison	69
10. Rouen — The Trial	74
11. Rouen — The Punishment	98
12. Joan's Secret Power	107
13. What Were Her Voices?	121
14. Analogous Powers, Ancient And Modern	140
15. Joan Of Arc And The Modern Psychic Movement	154
A Message	170
Translator's Note	173

TRANSLATOR'S PREFACE

UNTIL one has experienced it one can hardly realize the difficulty which lies in the adequate translation of a French book, dealing with a subtle and delicate subject. Only then does one understand that not only the words, but the whole method of thought and expression are different. A literal translation becomes impossibly jerky and staccato, while a paraphrase has to be very carefully done, if one has a respect for the original. M. Léon Denis has given me an entirely free hand in the matter, but I love and admire his book so much, that I earnestly desire to reproduce the text as closely as possible.

I should not have attempted the task were it not that, apart from the literary and historical aspects of the work, the psychic side is expounded by a profound student of such things, and calls therefore for some equivalent psychic knowledge upon the part of the translator. It is to be hoped, however, that the reader who is ignorant of psychic matters, or out of sympathy with them, will still be able to recognize the beauty of this picture done by one who had such love for his subject that he followed the maid every inch of the way from Domrémy to Rouen. M. Denis actually lives in Tours, and is familiar with Orleans, so that he has mastered the local colour in a most unusual way.

His treatment of his heroine is so complete that there is no need for me to say anything save to express my personal conviction that, next to the Christ, the highest spiritual being of whom we have any exact record upon this earth is the girl Jeanne. One would kneel rather than stand in her presence. We are particularly fortunate in the fact that we have fuller and more certain details of her life and character than of any celebrity in mediaeval or, perhaps, in modern history. The glorious life was so short and so public, that there was no time or place for shadows or misunderstandings.

It was spent under the very eyes of the world, and is recorded in the verbatim accounts of the most searching cross-examination that ever a woman endured, supplemented by an equally close enquiry when her character was rehabilitated a generation after her death. On that occasion over a hundred witnesses who had known her were put upon oath. Apart from the question of Christ's divinity, and comparing the two characters upon a purely human plane, there was much analogy between them. Each was sprung from the labouring class. Each proclaimed an inspired mission. Each was martyred while still young.

Each was acclaimed by the common people and betrayed or disregarded by the great. Each excited the bitter hatred of the church of their time, the high priests of which in each case conspired for their death. Finally, each spoke with the same simple definite phrases, short and strong, clear and concise. Jeanne's mission was on the surface warlike, but it really had the effect of ending a century of war, and her love and charity were so broad, that they could only be matched by Him who prayed for His murderers.

The text will show that M. Denis is an earnest student of psychic matters, with a depth of experience which forbids us to set his opinions easily aside. His other works, especially "Après la Mort," show how extensive have been his studies and how deep his convictions. There are portions of this work which bear traces of psychic influence, and he has even felt that at times he had some direct inspiration. This is a point which will seem absurd to some, and will cause even those who are sympathetic to suspend their judgment until they know more clearly what was the exact evidence which led M. Denis to such a conclusion. But if we omit or discount this personal claim there still remains a general statement which links Jeanne up with our modern psychic knowledge, finds a definite place for her therein, and succeeds for the first time—where Anatole France and others have failed—in giving us some intelligible reason for the obvious miracle that a girl of nineteen, who could neither read nor write, and knew nothing of military affairs, was able in a few months to turn the tide of a hundred years' war, and to save France from becoming a vassal of England.

Her achievement was attributed by herself (and she was the soul of truth) to her voices and her visions. It is M. Denis' task to show how these voices and visions fit into our present knowledge, and what were their most probable origin and meaning.

I have omitted those continual footnotes and references to authorities which prove M. Denis' accuracy and diligence but which break the narrative by drawing the reader's eyes forever to the bottom of the page. The serious student will find them in the original, and it will suffice in this version if it be stated that the main sources of information are to be found in the "Procès de Condamnation," the "Procès de Réhabilitation," Henri Martin's "Histoire de France," Delanne's "Fantômes des Vivants," Denis' "Aprés la Morte" and "Dans l'Invisible," Cagny's "Chronicles," "Chronique de la Pucelle," Quicherat's works, Anatole France's "Vie de Jeanne," Richers' "Histoire de la Pucelle," "Registres du Parlement," and other documents.

The beautiful literary touch of M. Denis would have won him fame, whatever topic engaged his pen, but he had very peculiar qualifications for this particular work, and though his views may be somewhat ahead of the present state of public knowledge and opinion, I am convinced that in the end his contribution to the discussion regarding Jeanne will prove to be the most important and the truest ever made. A great crisis of world thought and experience is at hand, and when it is past such views as those of M. Denis may form the basis upon which the reformed philosophies of the future will be based.

Arthur Conan Doyle.
April, 1924.

INTRODUCTION

THE memory of Jeanne d'Arc has never aroused such ardent and passionate controversies as have raged for the last few years round this great historical figure. One party, while exalting her memory, tries to monopolize her and to confine her personality within the limits of Catholic doctrine. A second, by means of tactics which are sometimes brutal, as in the case of Thalamas and Henri Bérenger, sometimes clever and learned, as in the case of M. Anatole France, tries to lessen her prestige and to reduce her mission to the proportions of an ordinary historical episode.

Where shall we find the truth as to the part played by Jeanne in history? As we read it, it is to be found neither in the mystic reveries of the men of faith nor in the material arguments of the positivists critics. Neither the one nor the other seems to hold the thread which form the mystery of this extraordinary life.

To penetrate the mystery of Jeanne d'Arc it seems to us necessary to study, and have practical knowledge of, psychic science. It is necessary to have sounded the depths of this invisible world, this ocean of life which envelops us, from which we all come at birth and into which we are replunged at death.

How can writers understand Jeanne if their thoughts have never risen above terrestrial facts, looked beyond the narrow horizon of an inferior material world, nor caught one glimpse of the life beyond?

During the last fifty years a whole series of manifestations and of discoveries have thrown a new light upon certain important aspects of life, of which we have had only vague and uncertain knowledge. By close observations and by methodical experiment in psychic phenomena a far-reaching science is gradually being built up.

The universe appears to us now as a reservoir of unknown forces of incalculable energy. An infinite vista dawns before our thoughts filled with forms and vital powers which escape our normal senses, though some manifestations of them have been measured with great precision by the aid of registering apparatus[1].

The idea of the supernatural fades away, and we see Nature herself rolling back for ever the horizon of her domain. The possibility of an invisible organized life, more rich and more intense than that of humanity, but regulated by tremendous laws, begins to intrude itself. This life in many cases impinges on our own and influences us for good or for evil.

Most of the phenomena of the past which have been asserted in the name of faith and denied in the name of reason can now receive a logical and scientific explanation. The extraordinary incidents scattered over the story of the maid of Orleans are of this order. Their comprehension is rendered the more easy by our knowledge of similar phenomena observed, classified and registered in our own time.

These can explain to us the nature of the forces which acted in and around her, guiding her life towards its noble end.

The historians of the nineteenth century, Michelet, Wallon, Quicherat, Henri Martin, Siméon Luce, Joseph Fabare, Vallet de Viriville, Lanéry d'Arc, have all agreed to exalt Jeanne as a marvelous heroine, and a sort of national Messiah. It is only in the twentieth century that the critical note has been heard. This has sometimes been bitter. M. Thalamas, Professor of the University, has even been accused by certain Catholic critics of treating this heroine as a wanton. He defends himself from this charge, and in his work "Jeanne d'Arc, History and Legend," he does not go beyond the limits of honest and courteous criticism. His point of view, however, is that of the materialist:

"It is not for us," he says, "who look on all genius as an affair of the nerves, to reproach Jeanne for having magnified into saints what was really the voice of her own conscience."

But sometimes in his lectures he was more severe. At Tours on April 29th, 1905, he reminded us of the opinion of Professor Robin on Jeanne d'Arc. She had never existed, he believed, and her whole story was a myth. M. Thalamas would not go so far as this, and recognized the reality of her life, but he attacked the deductions which her admirers had drawn from it. He exerted all his ingenuity to minimize what she had done without attacking her personal character. She had done nothing herself, or at least very little; for example, he held that it was the inhabitants of Orleans who had wrought their own deliverance.

Henri Bérenger and other writers have followed in the same sense, and the official view of the question seemed to be coloured by their theories. In the history books of the primary schools they have taken from the story of Jeanne everything which could have a psychic meaning. It is no longer a question of voices; it is always the voice of conscience which guides her. This difference is a very real one.

Anatole France in his artistic volumes does not go so far as this. He cannot get past the evidence as to the objective reality of the visions and of the voices. He is too well acquainted with the documentary evidence to deny that. His work is a faithful reconstruction of the epoch. The appearances of the towns, of the countryside, and of the men of that epoch are painted with the hand of a master and with a fineness of touch which recalls Renan. Yet reading him leaves one cold and disappointed. His judgments are often falsified by prejudice, and one is conscious, all through his pages, of a subtle and penetrating irony which is out of place in history.

In truth, an impartial judge may state that as Jeanne is exalted by the Catholics, she is attacked by the freethinkers less out of dislike for her than through a spirit of contradiction and of opposition. The heroine, dragged this way and that, becomes an object of contention to these rival parties. There is exaggerated statement on both sides, and the truth, as so often happens, is between the two extremes.

The vital question is the existence of occult forces, which the materialists ignore, of invisible powers which are not supernatural and miraculous, but which belong to those domains of Nature which have not yet been fully explored. Hence comes the inability to understand the work of Jeanne and the means by which it was possible for her to carry it out.

Her critics have never realized the immensity of the obstacles which the heroine had to surmount. A poor girl, eighteen years old, the daughter of humble peasants, without education, "knowing neither A nor B," says the Chronicle, she had against her, her own family, public opinion and all the world. What could she have accomplished without that inspiration, that vision of the world beyond, which sustained her?

Imagine this child of the fields in the presence of great lords, ladies, and prelates; in the court and in the camps. She was a simple rustic from the depths of the country, ignorant of warlike things, and speaking a provincial dialect! She had to meet the prejudices of rank and birth, and the pride of caste. Later she encountered the mockeries and the brutalities of soldiers accustomed to despise women, and unwilling to admit that a girl could command and direct them. In addition there was the hatred of the men of the Church, who in those days saw in everything which was unusual the intervention of the devil. They never pardoned her for acting independently of their authority, and indeed that was the main cause of her ruin.

Picture to yourself the prying curiosity of those debauched men amongst who she had to live constantly. She had to endure fatigue, long hours on horseback, and the crushing weight of iron armour. She had also to lie on the ground during weary nights in the camp, harassed by all the worries and responsibilities of her arduous task.

During her short career she surmounted all these obstacles, and out of a divided people split into a thousand factions, decimated by famine, and demoralized by all the miseries of a hundred years war, she built up a victorious nation.

It is this wonderful episode which clever but blind writers have tried to explain by purely material and terrestrial means, lame explanations which go to pieces when one realizes the facts! Poor blind souls—souls of the night, dazzled and dazed by the lights of the Beyond! It is to them that the words of a thinker apply:

"That which they know is nothing, but from what they do not know one could create a universe."

It is a deplorable thing that certain critics of our time feel impelled to minimize and drag down in a frenzy or dislike everything which rises above their own moral incapacity. Wherever a light shines, or a flame burns, one sees them running to pour water upon that which might give an illumination to humanity.

Jeanne, ignorant of human forces, but with profound psychic vision, gave them a magnificent lesson in the words which she addressed to the examiners at Poitiers, which are equally applicable to the modern skeptics, the little narrow minds of our generation:

"I read in a book where there are more things than are found in yours."

Learn to read there, also, you sceptics, and to understand these problems; then you may speak with a little more authority about Jeanne and her work.

When one studies the great scenes of history, one has to realize and reconstruct the souls of nations and of heroes. If you know how to love them they will come to you, these souls, and they will inspire you. It is the secret of the genius of history. That is what great writers like Michelet, Henri Martin, and others have done. They have gone out in sympathy to the genius of the race and of the era of which they wrote, and the breath of the Beyond runs through their pages. Others, like Anatole France, Lavisse, and his collaborators, remain dry and cold in spite of their cleverness, because they have no grasp of that personal intimate communion where soul reacts upon soul. This communion is the secret of all great artists, thinkers and poets. Without it there is no imperishable work.

A constant stream of inspiration flows down from the invisible world upon mankind. There are intimate ties between the living and the dead. All souls are united by invisible threads, and the more sensitive of us down here vibrate to the rhythm of the universal life. So was it with our heroine.

The critic may attack her memory; his efforts will never prevail. The story of the maid of Lorraine, like that of all the great agents of Providence, is graven on the eternal granite of history. Nothing can wipe out that record. It is one which indicates most clearly amid all the mixed tumult of life that sovereign hand which guides the world.

To understand this life, and to realize the power which guided it, one must raise one's mind to those great vital laws which govern the destiny of nations. Higher than all worldly events, and independent of the confused results of human action, one may trace an unswerving will which surmounts the resistance of individuals and works straight to the predestined end. Instead of losing itself in the confusion of life it seems rather to organize it, and to be the secret thread which leads through the maze. Gradually there appear a method and a system, which harmonize all things. Their inter-relation becomes more defined, while their contradictions fade away until one vast plan stands revealed. One realizes, then, that there is a latent invisible energy, reacting upon all of us, leaving to each certain measure of initiative, but enveloping all of us and sweeping us towards a fixed goal.

The apparent incoherences of life and of history depend upon the delicate equilibrium between the liberty of the individual and the authority of the

Supreme Law. The deeper workings of these forces dawn gradually upon the man who can penetrate into the inner meaning of things. If it were not for this profound law, there would be nothing but disorder and chaos in that infinite jumble of efforts and of individual ambitions which make up the workings of the human race.

From the days of Domrémy to those of Reims the action of this law could be traced in the whole episode of the Maid. During that period man was working for the most part in harmony with the higher Law. After the incident of the consecration at Reims, ingratitude, wickedness, the intrigues of courtiers and of clerics, and the bad conduct of the King obscured the issue. To quote the expression of Jeanne, "Men refused to do the will of God."

Selfishness, disorder and rapacity stood in the way of the higher action, which was attempted by Jeanne and her invisible helpers. The work of deliverance became more uncertain and was chequered by ill fortune and reverses. She followed out her mission none the less, but for its full accomplishment there would have been needed a greater length of time and ever harder exertions, with less disturbance from the forces of evil.

~

As I have said, it is entirely from the point of view of our new scientific knowledge that I undertake this work. I repeat it so that none may misunderstand my intention. In trying to throw a little light on the life of Jeanne d'Arc I am not actuated by any selfish motive or by any political or religious prejudice. My views are as far from those of the anarchists as from those of the reactionaries. I am neither among the blind fanatics, nor among those who are ever incredulous.

It is in the name of truth and of moral beauty, and out of love for our French Fatherland that I try to clear the noble figure of the inspired Maid from those shadows which have gathered round her.

Under the pretext of analysis and of free criticism there has been, as I have already remarked, a most regrettable tendency in our days to drag down everything which has been admired in the past, and to alter and to tarnish what has been spotless and perfect up to now.

It is a duty for any man, who can by pen or by voice exercise an influence on his fellows, to maintain and to defend whatever makes for the greatness of our country, and emphasizes the noble examples that she has given to the world, and the scenes of beauty which enrich her past and shed a glory on her history.

It is, on the other hand, an evil action to endeavour in any way to enfeeble our moral inheritance, the historical tradition of the people. Is it not the very thing which should give us strength in difficult hours? Is it not that which helps us to higher virility in moments of danger? The tradition of a people and its history are the poetry of its life, its solace in trouble, its hope in the future. It is by the common ties which it creates between all our citizens that we feel ourselves to be the children of the one mother and members of a common fatherland.

It is well that we should often recall the great scenes of our national history. It is full of striking lessons, and rich in wonderful examples. It is possibly superior in that respect to the history of any other nation. Wherever we explore the past of our race, everywhere and in every age we see great shadows hovering, and those shadows speak to us, and exhort us. From far- off centuries voices come down to us recalling great memories, memories which, if they were always present in our souls, would suffice to inspire and to brighten our lives. But there comes the chill wind of scepticism, of forgetfulness, and of indifference. The preoccupations of our material life absorb us, and we end by losing touch with all that has been most great and most eloquent in the teaching of the past. Among these traditions there is nothing more touching and more glorious than that which deals with this extraordinary young girl who illuminates the darkness of the Middle Ages by her radiant presence, and of whom Henri Martin has said, "Nothing like her has ever happened in the history of the world."

In the name of the past as well as of the future of our race, in the name of the work which still waits to be done, let us endeavour to keep in its entirety our moral inheritance. Let us try to keep from the soul of the people the intellectual poison which threatens it, and so to preserve for France that beauty and that strength which will make her great in hours of peril and restore to her all that prestige and self-respect which have been weakened by so many evil and sophistical theories.

∼

It is only fair to recognize that the Catholic world—of recent years, at any rate—has done solemn homage to Jeanne. The orthodox have praised her, have glorified her, and have raised statues and temples in her honour. On the other hand, the Republican thinkers have discussed a project of founding a national fête in her honour, which should be dedicated to the cult of patriotism. But neither party has really understood the true character of our heroine, nor grasped the inner meaning of her life. There are few men who have been in a position to analyze this great figure who stands so high above the days in which she lived, and seems more and more majestic as the years roll by.

There is in this wonderful life a depth which cannot be plumbed by minds which are not prepared beforehand for such a study. There are factors which must cause uncertainty and confusion in the thoughts of those who have not the necessary gifts to solve this great problem. Hence the sterile discussions and the vain polemics. But for the man who has lifted the veil of the invisible world the life of Jeanne is brilliantly clear. Her whole story becomes at once rational and intelligible.

Observe how many different points of view and contradictory ideas there are among those who praise the heroine! Some try to find in her some argument for their particular party. Others strive to draw some secular moral from her fate. Some again only wish to see in the triumph of Jeanne the exaltation of popular and patriotic sentiment. One may well ask if in this devotion which rises from all France there is not blended much which is egotistical and much which is mixed with self-interest. No doubt they think of Jeanne, and no doubt they love Jeanne, but at the same time, are they not thinking more of themselves and of their parties? Do they not search in that glorious life only for that which may flatter their own personal feelings, their own political opinions, or their own unavowed ambitions? There are not many, I fear, who raise themselves above prejudice and above the interests of caste or of class. Few, indeed, try to penetrate the secret of this life, and among those who have penetrated, no one up to now, save in a most guarded way, has dared to speak out and to tell that which he saw and understood.

As for me, if my claims for speaking of Jeanne d'Arc are modest ones, there is at least one which I can confidently make. It is that I am free from every prejudice and from all desire either to please or to displease. With thoughts free, and conscience independent, searching and wishing for nothing but truth, thus is it that I approach this great subject, and search for that mysterious clue which is the secret of her incomparable career.

---

1. Annales des Sciences psychiques, August, September, October 1907, February 1909.

1

DOMRÉMY

I AM a son of Lorraine, born like Jeanne in the valley of the Meuse, and my infancy was full of the memories which she had left in that country.

During my youth I often visited the place where she lived. I loved to wander under the great vaults of our Lorraine woods, which are the remains of the ancient forests of the Gauls. Like her, I have many times listened to the harmonies of the fields and of the waste places, and I can claim that I too know the mysterious voices of space, those voices which, when one is alone, convey inspiration to the thinker and bring him into touch with the eternal verities.

In my manhood I have followed across France the traces of her footsteps. I have made almost stage by stage the same tragic journey. I have seen the castle of Chinon where she was received by Charles VII, although it is now but a ruin. I have seen deep in Touraine the little Church of Fierbois whence she recovered the sword of Charles Martel, and the caves of Courtineau in which she took refuge during the storm.

Then, too, I have seen Orleans and Reims and Compiègne where she was taken. There is not one place that she has passed where I have not meditated, prayed and mourned. Later, in this city of Rouen, above which her great presence seems still to hover, I terminated my pilgrimage. Like those Christians who walk step by step along the path which leads to Calvary I have followed the melancholy road which led the great martyr to her doom.

More recently I returned to Domrémy. I saw once again the humble cottage where she was born, the chamber with its narrow window where her virginal body, destined to so tragic a fate, has brushed the walls, the rustic press where she kept her belongings and the place where, in her ecstasy, she heard the voices. Then, too, I saw the church where she so often prayed. Thence, by the road which climbs the hill, I made my way to the holy place where she loved to dream. I saw the vine which belonged to her father, the Fairy tree, and the sweetly murmuring fountain. The cuckoo sang in the hoary wood. The scent of the pine trees floated in the air. The breeze shook the foliage and murmured in the depths of the thickets. At my feet were spread the laughing fields covered with flowers and watered by the windings of the Meuse.

Opposite, the hill of Julien rose abruptly, reminding one of the Roman period and of the apostate Caesar; in the distance, wooded hills and deep valleys alternated to the hazy horizon. A deep sweetness, a peaceful serenity brooded over the whole of this country. It was truly a blessed place conducive to thought, a place where the vague harmonies of heaven seemed to mix with the gentle and distant murmurs of human life. Oh, dreaming soul of Jeanne, I tried hard to share the feelings which came to you, and I found them deep and real. They surged into my own spirit; they filled me with a poignant rapture. And your whole life, that dazzling record, unrolled itself before my thoughts like a glorious panorama ending in an apotheosis of fire. For one moment I seemed to have actually lived this life, and that which my heart felt no human pen can describe.

Behind me, an obtrusive monument and a discordant note in the symphony of subtle impressions, there rose the church and the theatrical group where Jeanne is seen on her knees at the feet of S. Michael and of two gilded Saints. The statue of Jeanne alone, rich in expression, touches one, interests one, and holds one's attention. A name is carved on the pedestal, that of Allar—himself a mystic.

At some distance from Domrémy, on a steep slope in the midst of the woods, lies the modest chapel of Bermont. Jeanne used to come here every week. She would follow the path which from Greux winds on to the plateau, passes under the trees and leads to the fountain of Thiébault. She would climb the hill in order to keel before the ancient Madonna whose statue, dating from the eighth century, is still held in veneration. I walked, heavy with thought, along this picturesque path, and I traversed these tangled woods where the birds sing. The whole country is full of Celtic reminiscences. Our fathers have raised there an altar of stone. These sacred fountains and these gloomy shadows were once the witnesses of the Druidical ceremonies. The soul of Gaul lives and vibrates in such places. Without doubt it spoke to the heart of Jeanne, even as she speaks to-day to the heart of her fellow- countrymen and of those who understand her.

I went further. I wished to see everything which had

to do with the life of Jeanne and everything which recalled her memory. There is Vouthon where her mother was born, and the little village of Burey, which still contains the dwelling of her uncle, Durand Laxart, he who helped her on her mission by leading her to Vaucouleurs and into the presence of the Lord of Baudricourt. The humble house is still there, with the carving of lilies decorating the threshold, but it has been changed into a stable. A rude chain holds the door. I undid it, and as I looked in a goat huddled in the shadows of the corner uttered its thin and plaintive bleating.

I wandered all over this country, lost in my dreams, as I stood by the places which meant so much in the infancy of Jeanne. I traversed the narrow valleys, hemmed in by dark forests which open out from the Meuse. I stood lost in thought in the solitude at evening time, at the hour when the nightingale sings, and when the stars first gleam in the depths of the heavens. I listened to all the vague sounds and the mysterious voices of Nature. In these places I felt myself far from man with an invisible world close beside me.

Then it was that a prayer came from the depth of my being; then it was that I evoked the spirit of Jeanne. Immediately I seemed to feel the strength and the sweetness of her presence. The air vibrated. There was a sense of brightness around me. Invisible wings seemed to be beating in the dusk. An unknown melody floated down from above, lulled my senses and drew tears to my eyes.

And the Angel of France inspired me with words which I here piously repeat, even as I received them:

"Your soul rises up and is conscious at this moment of the protection which God throws over you. May your heart take courage, you who love and desire to serve our dear France, that France which I look upon always as a protector and a mother with love and devotion. I was a simple Christian upon earth. I feel here in the Beyond the same emotions, the same need for prayer, but it is my wish that my memory be free and detached from all earth interests. I only give my heart and my remembrance to those who see in me the humble daughter of God, loving all those who live in this land of France and striving to inspire them with sentiments of love, of justice and of courage."

2

THE SITUATION IN 1429

WHAT was the situation of France in the fifteenth century, at the moment when Jeanne d'Arc appeared on the great stage of history?

The war against England had lasted for a hundred years. In four successive defeats the French nobility had been crushed and almost annihilated. From Cressy to Poitiers, and from the field of Agincourt to that of Verneuil, our chivalry had strewn the ground with its dead. The survivors had split into two rival parties whose quarrels enfeebled and desolated France. The Duke of Orleans had been assassinated by the retainers of the Duke of Burgundy, who in turn met his death a little later at the hands of the Armagnacs.

All this went on under the very eyes of the enemy, who advanced step by step, invading the Northern Provinces. He had already for many years occupied La Guyenne. After a desperate resistance, in the course of a siege which surpassed in horror anything that the imagination could conceive, Rouen had been compelled to surrender. Paris, the population of which had been decimated by sickness and famine, was in the hands of the English. The Loire saw the enemy upon its banks. Orleans, the capture of which would mean that the stranger had seized the very heart of France, still held out, but for how long?

Vast stretches of our country had been turned into desert. Cultivation had ceased. The villages were abandoned. One only saw weeds and thistles in the fields and the charred ruins of burnt houses. Everywhere were the traces of the ravages of war, death and desolation.

The inhabitants of the country, in desperation, concealed themselves in caves. Others took refuge in the hills of the Loire, or sought protection in the towns, where they died of famine. Often to escape the soldiers these wretched people sought safety in the woods, organized themselves into bands and became as cruel as the brigands from whom they had fled. Wolves wandered round the outskirts of the towns, penetrated into them at night and devoured the corpses which had been left without burial. Such was "La grande pitié qui est au royaume de France," as her voices described it to Jeanne.

Poor Charles VI in his madness had signed the Treaty of Troyes which disinherited his son and made Henry of England heir to the throne. And so in the Cathedral of St. Denis, over the grave of the mad King, a herald proclaimed Henry of Lancaster to be King both of France and of England.

The bodies of our Kings lying under the heavy slabs of their tombs may well have palpitated with shame and grief. The Dauphin Charles, dispossessed and called in derision "King of Bourges," sank into a state of discouragement and lethargy. He lacked both resources and bravery. His courtiers treated in secret with the enemy. He himself planned to fly to Scotland or to Spain, renouncing the throne to which he thought that possibly he was not entitled, for he had his own doubts as to the legitimacy of his birth. One heard on all sides the lamentable plaint, the cry of agony from a people who were being thrust by the conquerors into their grave. France felt herself to be lost, and she was struck to the heart. A few more blows and she would descend into the great silence of death. What help could possibly come to her? No earthly power could accomplish such a miracle as the resurrection of a people who had lost all hope. But it is another power, an invisible one, which watches over the destiny of nations. At the moment when everything seemed to have crumbled it was this power which brought to a despairing people its redemption. Certain signs seemed to announce its coming.

Among these signs a visionary, Marie of Avignon, had forced herself into the presence of the King. She had seen, she said, in her trances a suit of armour which heaven was reserving for a young girl destined to save the Kingdom.

On all sides one heard the ancient prophecy of Merlin which announced that a virgin liberator would come from a chestnut wood.

And then, like a ray from Heaven in the midst of this night of desolation and of misery, Jeanne appeared.

Hark! Hark! From the depths of the fields and the forests of Lorraine, one hears the gallop of her horse. She is coming! She is coming to reanimate this despairing people, to renew their lost courage, to direct their resistance, to save France from death.

3

THE INFANCY OF JOAN OF ARC

AT the foot of the hills at the side of the Meuse a few cottages were grouped round a modest church. Green meadows, rising and falling, stretched away from them and the little river with its clear waters ran past them. On the slopes above them lay cultivated fields and vineyards, stretching up to the deep forest which rose like a wall across de summit of the hills, a forest full of mysterious murmurs and the singing of the birds. Out of it came suddenly, from time to time, wolves, the terror of the flocks; or soldiers, brigands and robbers, more dangerous than the wild beasts.

This was Domrémy, a village hitherto unknown, but which was to be famous throughout the whole world, on account of the child born there in 1412.

To recall the history of this young girl is ever the best means of refuting the arguments of her enemies. That I will now do—bringing out, I hope, certain facts which have remained in the shadow, some of which have been revealed to me by psychic means.

Many works—masterpieces of research and of

learning—have been written on the Maid of Lorraine. Far be it from me to pretend to equal them! But this book is distinguished by one characteristic trait. It is illuminated here and there by the very thoughts of the heroine. Thanks to messages obtained from her, the authenticity of which is absolutely satisfying, these pages become in part an echo of her own voice, and of the voices of the Beyond. It is for this reason that it has a claim upon the attention of the reader.

~

Jeanne was not of high birth. The daughter of poor labourers, she spun wool by the side of her mother, or shepherded the flock in the fields of the Meuse when she was not accompanying her father to the plough.

She did not know how to read or write. She was absolutely ignorant of everything connected with war. She was a sweet and good child, loved by all, especially by the poor and the wretched, whom she was for ever helping and consoling. To illustrate this there are some touching anecdotes. She willingly gave up her bed to some weary pilgrim, and passed the night on a bundle of straw in order to give repose to old folk tired by a long journey. She nursed the sick, as in the case of Simon Musnier, her neighbour, who was prostrated with fever, laying him on her couch, and watching over him during the night.

She was a dreamer, and loved in the evenings to watch the stars break out in the skies, or to follow during the day the changes of light and shade. The sound of the wind in the branches and in the thickets, the murmur of the springs, and all the harmonies of Nature, enchanted her. But most of all, she loved the sound of bells. It was to her like a greeting from Heaven to earth, and when in the peaceful eventide, far from the village in some little valley where her flock was gathered, she heard their silvery notes, their slow and calm vibrations making her hour of her return, she would fall into a sort of ecstasy, into a long prayer in which her whole soul reached out towards Heaven. In spite of her poverty, she found the means of giving little gifts to the bell-ringer of the village, in order that he might continue the peal of his bells longer than usual.

Full of the intuition that her coming on earth was for some great object, her thoughts plunged into the depths of the invisible, trying to trace the path on which should go.

"She searched her own mind," Henri Martin tells us.

Whilst the souls of her companions were imprisoned in their fleshly garb, her whole being lay open to high influences. In the hour of sleep her spirit, freed from material ties, flowed out into the etheric spaces. There it strengthened itself in the powerful currents of life and of love, and on awakening preserved some intuition of its experience. Thus, little by little, her psychic faculties awoke and grew. Soon they were to be brought into action.

Meanwhile these impressions and these dreams did not lessen her love for work. Assiduous in her tasks, she did all that was possible to satisfy her parents and everyone else with whom she had to do. "There is no blessing like work," said she later, for she had experience that work is the best friend of man, his helper, his counsellor in life, his consoler in adversity, and that there is no true happiness without it. "Vive labeur," is the motto which her family adopted and inscribed on her shield when the King included her in the ranks of the nobility.

Even in the little details of life Jeanne showed a keen sense of duty, a sure judgment and a clear vision, which rendered her superior to all those around her. One could already see in her a wonderful soul, one of those deep and passionate spirits which come down upon earth to carry out a great mission. A mysterious influence surrounded her. Voices spoke in her ears and in her heart. Invisible being inspired her, directed her acts, and guided her steps. What was it that these voices commanded? Imperious orders were given to her from the Beyond. She was to give up this life of peace. This poor child, seventeen years of age, was to dare the tumult of the camps, at a time when too often soldiers were mere bandits. She was to quit all—her village, her father and her mother, her flock, everything that she loved —to hasten to the help of agonized France. To the good people of Vaucouleurs who pitied her lot, she answered, "It is for this that I was born."

∽

The first vision came in the summer-time at mid-day. The sky was cloudless, and the sun poured down upon the widespread fields. Jeanne was praying in the garden which stretched from her father's house down to the church. She heard a voice which said to her, "Jeanne, daughter of God, be good and wise. Frequent the church[1]. Put your confidence in the Lord." She was terrified, but raising her eyes she saw in a dazzling light an angelic figure full of strength and sweetness surrounded by other radiant forms.

On another day the Archangel, S. Michael, and the

Saints who accompanied him spoke of the state of the country and revealed to her, her mission.

"It is necessary that you go to the help of the Dauphin, so that through you he may recover his Kingdom."

Jeanne, taken aback, excused herself.

"I am only a poor girl and I know neither how to write nor how to fight."

"Daughter of God, go. I will be your help," the voice replied to her.

Little by little her interviews with the spirits became more frequent. They were never of long duration. Counsels from on high are always brief, to the point, and luminous. That is clearly shown by her replies to those who questioned her at Rouen: "What doctrine did S. Michael teach you?" they asked her.

"He always said, 'Be a good child, and God will help you.'"

This is both simple and sublime and sums up all the law of life. High spirits do not dissipate their energy in long speeches. Even to-day those who can communicate with the higher realms of the Beyond only receive teaching which is condensed and marked with high wisdom. Jeanne added: "S. Michael has told me to be good and to frequent the Church."

So it is in the case of every soul who aspires to good. Rectitude and prayer are the first conditions of a true and pure life.

One day S. Michael said to her, "Daughter of God, you will lead the Dauphin to Reims, so that he may receive his Consecration."

S. Catherine and S. Margaret said to her continually, "Go! Go! We will help you."

Thus there was established between Jeanne and her guides close relations. From her "Brothers of Paradise" she drew the necessary courage to carry out her work. She was filled with the idea. France awaited her. She must go.

～

In the early dawn of a winter day Jeanne rose. She had prepared her light baggage—a small packet—and her staff. Then she went to kneel at the foot of the bed where her father and mother were still lying. Weeping silently she murmured a farewell. At this sad moment she may well recalled the kindness and the cares of her mother and the troubles of her father, whose brow was already wrinkled with age. She may have thought of the gap which her departure would cause, and the grief of all those whose life and joys and troubles she had always shared. But duty called her. She must not fail in her task.

Adieu, poor parents, adieu, you have had so many uneasy thoughts as to the fate of your daughter, who in your dreams you have seen in the company of men-at-arms.

She will not conduct herself as you have feared, for she is pure, pure as the spotless lily. Her heart knows one love—that of her country.

"Good-bye, I am going to Vaucouleurs," she said as she passed before the cottage of the labourer, Gerard, whose family was related to her own.

"Good-bye, Mengette," said she to her companion.

"Good-bye, you, too, with whom up to now I have lived so happily."

There was only one friend whom she avoided at this moment of farewell, that was her dear Hauviette. Leaving her would have been too trying. Jeanne, no doubt, already felt herself somewhat shaken, and she had need of all her courage.

She left for Beurey where one of her uncles lived, intending to go thence to Vaucouleurs, and so on to the Court. At seventeen years of age one pictures her traveling alone under the vast vault of Heaven, along a road sown with dangers. And Domrémy never saw her more.

---

1. At this epoch the Catholic religion was the most wide- spread religious form, and almost the only one which could unite souls to God. That is why the spirit who called himself S. Michael conformed with the views of that particular time, in order the better to attain his end. AUTHOR'S NOTE.

4

VAUCOULEURS

FROM that day onwards difficulty after difficulty had to be surmounted, and these difficulties were more cruel, because they were raised by those from whom she might well have expected sympathy, affection and help. One may apply to her the words, "She has come among her own, and her own knew her not."

Jeanne was faced with painful alternatives from the beginning to the end of her mission. At the outset she, who has so submissive to the authority of her parents and so attached to her duty, was compelled, in spite of the love which she bore her father and her mother, to disregard their orders, and secretly to fly from the house in which she had been born.

Her father had had in a dream the revelation of her plans. One night he dreamed that his daughter was quitting her country and her family, and riding off with men-at-arms [1]. He was much troubled over this and spoke to his sons about it, ordering them, rather than allow such a thing, to drown their sister in the Meuse. "If you won't do it," he added, "I will!"

Jeanne had to dissimulate, being resolved that she would obey God rather than man.

At Rouen her judges put painful and searching questions to her over this.

"Do you thing it was right," they asked her, "to leave your father and your mother without a word of farewell?"

"I have obeyed my father and my mother in everything else. Since I left them I have had letters written to them and they have pardoned me."

In this she showed her deference and her submission to those who brought her up. None the less, the judges insisted:

"When you left your father and your mother, did you not feel that you were committing a sin?"

Jeanne laid her whole thoughts bare in this beautiful reply:

"Since God commanded it, I had to do it. If I had had a hundred fathers and a hundred mothers, and if I had been the daughter of the King, I should, none the less, have left them."

She was accompanied by one of her uncles, Durand Lexart, whom she had picked up in passing through Beurey. He was the only member of her family who knew of her intentions, and the only one who had encouraged her in her plans. She then presented herself to Robert de Baudricourt, who held Vaucouleurs for the Dauphin. Her first reception was brutal. Jeanne was not discouraged. She had been warned of it by her Voices. Her resolution was adamant. Nothing could turn her from her object. She stated it in the strongest terms to the good people of Vaucouleurs.

"Before mid-Lent I must be with the King, even though I wear my legs down to the knees in getting there."

And little by little the rude soldier was led by her insistence to pay more attention to that which she proposed.

Like all those who approached her, Robert de Baudricourt felt the power of this young girl. After having had her exorcised by Jean Tournier, Curé of Vaucouleurs, and being convinced that there was no evil in her, he dared no longer deny her mission, or throw obstacles in her way, but gave her a horse and an escort.

The knight, Jean de Metz, carried away by the ardour of Jeanne, had already promised to take her to the King.

"When shall I do it?" he asked her.

She replied eagerly, "Better to-day than to-morrow, better tomorrow than later."

She left at last, and the final order of the Captain of Vaucouleurs was, "Go, and we will see what comes of it," a half-hearted and discouraging farewell.

What did it matter to Jeanne? It was not the voices of the earth that she hearkened to, it was to those from on high, the voices which strengthened and sustained her.

In her soul, strength and confidence increased amid the uncertainties and perils which each day brought. Often she repeated the proverb of her country: "Aid yourself and God will aid you."

Her future was threatening. Everywhere around her there was cause for alarm, but within was the Divine driving force.

Surely here is an example which she has given to all the pilgrims of life. The road of mankind is lined with the ambushes of Fate. Everywhere are traps and pitfalls. To help us in our difficulties God has implanted in us latent energies which we can use by drawing to us these mysterious powers, these helpers from on high who increase a hundredfold our personal strength and assure us of success in the struggle. "Aid yourself and God will aid you."

She started, accompanied only by a few brave men. She journeyed day and night. She had to pass a hundred and fifty leagues through hostile provinces to reach Chinon, where the Dauphin Charles was in residence, he whom they named in contempt, "King of Bourges," since he only reigned now over a little slip of his own Kingdom. Charles, forever trying to forget his evil fortune by devoting himself to pleasure, was surrounded by couriers who betrayed him and treated in secret with the enemy.

She had to pass the country of Burgundy, the ally of England, and to make her way in rainy weather by secret paths across the fords of flooded rivers, lying at night on the cold and wet earth. Jeanne never hesitated. Her Voices said to her continually, "Go, Daughter of God, go. We will come to your aid."

And she went. She went in spite of obstacles, in spite of dangers. She was flying to the help of her prince, who was himself without either hope or courage.

But what a marvelous situation! Here is a child coming to draw France out of the abyss. What does she bring with her for the task? Is it military aid? Is it an army? No, nothing of the sort! What she brings is simply faith in herself, faith in the future of France, that faith which exalts the soul and which can move mountains. What did Jeanne herself say to all those who met her on her journey? "I come from the King of Heaven and I will bring you the help of Heaven."

---

1. This veridical dream seems to show that Jeanne's psychic power was to some extent hereditary.—TRANSLATOR'S NOTE.

5

CHINON, POITIERS AND TOURS

MOST authors think that Jeanne entered Touraine at Amboise, following the Roman road which skirts the left bank of the Loire. In that case she would have come from Gient to Blois, passing through Sologne. Leaving Amboise she would have passed the Cher at S. Martin le Beau, and then would have halted at St. Catherine de Fierbois, where there was a sanctuary consecrated to one of her Saints. According to an old tradition, Charles Martel, having conquered the Saracens, and exterminated them in the wild woods in the midst of which this Chapel was built (Ferus Boscus-Fierbois), left his sword in the oratory. Rebuild in 1375, it was frequented by knights and men-at-arms who, in the hope of getting cured from their wounds, would vow to make a pilgrimage and to leave their swords there.

On the road an ambush had been laid by a band of ruffians, who had probably been directed by the treacherous La Trémoille, and were charged to carry off Jeanne. But at the sight of her these bandits seem to have stood helpless before her and to have let her pass.

According to the evidence of Poulengy and of Novelonpont, each corroborating the other, the journey from Vaucouleurs to Chinon was performed in eleven days.

"It follows," says the Abbé Bosseboeuf, "that she arrived on Wednesday, the 23rd February." Wallon, Quicherat, and others put it as the 6th of March.

At last she sighted the town with its three castles, all grouped together in one long grey mass of crenelated walls, towers and castle keeps.

At her entry into Chinon the little caravan passed through the narrow streets between Gothic houses, their fronts faced with slates and decorated at each corner with wooden statues. One can imagine how marvelous stories at once began to circulate from mouth to mouth among the folk who gathered in the evenings, in the circle of light thrown by the torches above the doors, about this young girl who had come from the frontiers of Lorraine in order to carry out the prophecies and to put an end to the insolent victories of the English.

Jeanne and her escort took up their lodgings at the house "of a good woman near the castle."

No doubt this was the house of Signor Reignier de la Barre, whose widow and daughter received the Maid with joy. There she remained for two days without obtaining audience of the Prince. Later she lodged in the castle itself, in the tower of Coudray.

This audience which she had so longed for was at last granted to her. It was evening. The glare of torches, the sound of the trumpets, and all the pomp of the reception could not dazzle or intimidate her. She had come from a world more dazzling than ours. She had known of glories to which all that we could show her are pale indeed—farther away than Domrémy, farther away than the earth. In ages which preceded her birth, she had been familiar with assemblies more glorious than the Court of France, and she had preserved within her the intuition.

Louder than the clash of arms and the blare of trumpets, she heard a voice which spoke within her, and which repeated, "Go, Daughter of God, I am with you."

Among my readers some may find that what I say seems strange. Let me remind them that spirit existed before the body, that it has experienced before its last terrestrial birth vast periods of time during which it has filled many parts, and that it re-descends into this world at each new incarnation with the whole accumulation of qualities, of faculties and of aptitudes which were formed in that dim past which it has experienced.

There is in each of us, deep down in the depths of our conscience, an accumulation of impressions and of memories springing from our former lives, whether led upon earth or in the Beyond. These remembrances slumber within us. The heavy mantle of flesh stifles them, and holds them down, but sometimes under the impulse of some external pressure, they suddenly awake and intuitions come to the surface. Faculties which we have ignored reappear, and for an instant we become a very different being from that which others have up to that moment known.

You have seen, no doubt, those plants which float on the surface of the stagnant water of ponds. They form an image of the human soul. It floats over the dark depths of its own past. Its roots go back to unknown and distant attachments, whence it draws the vital sap and produces an ephemeral flower which can open, spread itself out and bloom for a time in the fields of our terrestrial life.

~

In the immense hall of the castle to which Jeanne was led, there were assembled three hundred lords, knights and noble ladies in brilliant costumes.

What an impression such an experience might be expected to produce on a humble shepherdess! What courage was needed to face all these licentious or critical eyes, and this crowd of courtiers who she felt to be hostile to herself!

There was present Regnault de Chartres, Chancellor of France and Archbishop of Reims, a prelate with a hard, perfidious and envious nature; there was La Trémoille, Court Chancellor, a dark, jealous man who dominated the King and plotted in secret with the English. There was the hard and arrogant Raoul de Gaucourt, Grand Master of the King's household. There was Marshal Gilles de Retz, the wicked magician, better known under the nickname of "Bluebeard."

Then there were titled harlots and cunning, avaricious priests. Jeanne felt all around her an atmosphere of incredulity and hostility. Such was the Court in which Charles VII lived, weakened by his abuse of pleasure, far from the seat of war, and surrounded by his favourites and his mistresses.

Suspicious and critical, the King, in order to test Jeanne, caused his throne to be occupied by one of his courtiers, and concealed himself in the crowd. But she went straight to him, knelt down before him and spoke to him for a long time in a low voice. She revealed to him his secret thoughts, his doubts as to his own birth, "and the face of this sad monarch lit up with a ray of confidence and of faith."

This aroused interest and amazement, for all felt that an extraordinary phenomenon had been produced. But still there was no one there who could believe that the fate of the proudest kingdom of Christianity could lie in such hands as these, or that the feeble arm of a poor village girl could be ordained to carry out a task which had been unsuccessfully attempted by the counsels of the most wise and by the courage of the most brave.

∽

Sent on to Poitiers, Jeanne appeared there before a Commission of Enquiry composed of twenty theologians, including two bishops, those of Poitiers and of Maguelonne.

"It was a wonderful sight," said Alain Chartier, writing under the immediate impression of the scene, "to see this woman disputing with so many men, ignorant among the learned and alone among her enemies."

All her answers showed great vivacity and extraordinary tact. She broke out continually into unforeseen and original remarks which made the pitiable objections of her examiners seem ridiculous. The actual record of the Interrogatory of Poitiers has been destroyed. Some historians lay the responsibility of this upon the agents of the Crown of France, who showed so much ingratitude and so much wicked indifference towards the Maid during her long captivity. There only remains to us a résumé of the conclusion at which these doctors arrived who were summoned to give their opinion of Jeanne.

"In her," they said, "we find no evil, but much good, humility, purity, devotion, honesty and simplicity."

We have also the witnesses who gave evidence in the Process of Rehabilitation. Brother Séquin of the Order of Preaching Friars expressed himself thus, with simplicity and good humour:

"I asked Jeanne what dialect her voices spoke.'

"A better one than yours," she answered me.

"And as a matter of fact, I speak a Limousin dialect.

"Going on with my questions, I said to her, 'Do you believe in God?'

"'A good deal more than you do,' she answered."

Another of these Poitiers judges, William Amery, said to her, "You say that God promised you victory, and yet you are asking for soldiers. What is the good of soldiers if victory is already promised?"

"The soldiers," said Jeanne, "will fight in the name of God and the God will give victory."

When they asked her for signs, that is to say, for miracles:

"I have not come to Poitiers to give signs, but take me to Orleans, and that will show you what I am sent for."

She had after this to undergo an examination of matrons presided over by the Queen of Sicily.

Emerging triumphantly from all these tests she still had to wait more than a month before she could march against the English, for it was only at the critical moment, when the situation of Orleans had become truly desperate, that Dunois obtained permission to take her as a last resource at the head of a convoy of supplies.

John went on to Tours to get her armour and her Standard. The town was greatly excited at the moment. The citizens were working hard at the fortifications. On October 14th, 1428, Marshal Gaucourt, Baillie of Orleans, and Grand Master of the King's Household, told them that the English had laid siege to Orleans, and that they would next march upon Tours. The City was putting itself into a state of defence. "In every part," says the Chronicle, "masons and artisans were hard at work." They laboured hard to deepen and enlarge the moats and to prepare the defences of the bridges. On the towers and along the ramparts they threw up wooden shelters for the watchers. They practiced their artillery and gathered into the town bombards and culverins, with gunpowder, balls of stone, and everything else which pertained to gunnery at the period. Let the enemy come! They would know how to receive him.

The ancient city of Tours was at that time a most important place. They called it "the Second Rome" on account of its numerous churches, its monasteries, and above all its Shrine of St. Martin, to which folk came from every part of Christendom.

In order to understand the surroundings at the time of Jeanne d'Arc let us climb in imagination to the summit of one of the towers of the sanctuary of St. Martin, the tower of Charlemagne, for example, which remains up to our own time, and which encloses the tomb of Luitgarde, wife of Charlemagne, whence it takes its name.

The aspect of the town, from a bird's-eye point of view, would resemble very much that of the other great French cities of the Middle Ages, and so it might be well to pause here for a few moments and describe it.

The fortifications formed four unbroken lines of walls and towers. Inside the walls was a labyrinth of narrow streets and cramped squares lined by long rows of houses with high gables and irregular roofs, each story projecting above the other. There were statues on either side of the doors upon sculptured supports, and high dormer windows of stained glass. To complete the picturesque effect one has to imagine grotesque iron signs taking the place of the numbers of the houses and swinging in the wind. Some of them would have an historical or heraldic meaning, others would be emblematic, commemorative or religious. Here, for example, in the Grande Rue were the signs of the Unicorn, of the Magpie, and of the Golden Paternoster. In the Place St. Martin there were the signs of the Preaching Ape and the Yowling Cat. In the Rue de la Rôtisserie there was the sign of the Three Tortoises, and so on.

From the high point on which we stand we would look down upon a forest of sharp pinnacles, belfries and walls, from which emerge the three masses of the Cathedral, the central portion only in course of building, so that the towers are not as yet more than from thirty to sixty feet above the ground. There, too, is the Abbey of St. Julien, and the far more imposing mass of the Shrine of St. Martin, only two towers of which remain to-day.

At our feet lies the city with its fifty churches and chapels, its eight great walled cloisters, its numerous inns and dwellings of the nobles. There is a whole forest of spires, pinnacles, belfries, clustered towers and high Gothic chimneys. Then you see a maze of streets which cross and re-cross, and narrow squares crowded with people and horses. Listen to the murmur, to the low roar of the city which mounts to your ears! Hark to the tolling of the hours which sounds from all the bells!

Now imagine one clear ray of sunshine falling upon this scene. See the river with all its changing tints!

Further off is the countryside covered with vines and great forests which flourish upon the two plateaus, especially the one to the south, and form a verdant frame around the city gleaming at the bottom of the valley. Realise all that, and you will have some idea of the appearance of Tours on the day when Jeanne d'Arc, followed by her military escort, made her entrance.

According to the deposition at the trial of her page, Louis de Contes, she lodged with a lady named Lapau. From the evidence of her almoner, Jean Pasquerel, it was with a citizen, Jean Dupuy, that she stayed. These contradictions are only apparent. As a matter of fact, the Tourainian noble, Jehan du Puy, had for wife Eleanor de Paul, but after the fashion in those days the name was contracted. When requested by Queen Yolande to give hospitality to a strange guest, who she had taken under her protection, Jean du Puy, counsellor to the King, with his wife received her into their house situated near the Church of St. Pierre. Many archaeologists believe it to have been the house which we now call Tristan.

It was at Tours that Brother Pasquerel, reader at the Augustinian Convent in the town, was attached to the service of Jeanne as almoner. He followed her faithfully up to the time of her capture at Compiègne one year later.

It was at Tours also that the brave child received her military outfit, her sword and her banner. Following her instructions an armourer of the town went to look for the sword deposited by Charles Martel at St. Catherine de Fierbois. It was disinterred from behind the altar, and no one else in the world had known that it was there. For our heroine, therefore, this sword sprang forth from the dust of the centuries in order once again to chase the invader from France. Another armourer of Tours built a brilliant suit of steel armour for Jeanne.

Following the instructions of her Voices, Jeanne had a white banner made by an artist of Touraine to serve as a Standard and as a rallying point. It was embroidered with a silk fringe and bore on it an image of God blessing the Lilies of France, with the motto, "Jesus Maria." The heroine never separated the cause of France from that higher One, the Divine Inspiration, whence her mission came.

Jeanne left Tours about the 25th April, 1429 for Blois, where the war chiefs and the main body of the army were awaiting her. Twelve days later, a date of imperishable memory, she gained the battle of Tourelle and raised the siege of Orleans.

When she quitted Tours all the population gathered in the streets and open spaces to see and to hail her.

She caracoled lightly on her beautiful war-horse in her white armour, which shone in the morning sun. With her banner in her hand and the sword of Fierbois at her side, she was all radiant with hope and faith. She seemed the very Angel of War come down as a messenger from on high.

6

ORLEANS

THE journey from Tours to Orleans was one long ovation. Everywhere Jeanne raised hope and confidence as she passed. If the courtiers suspected and despised her, the people at least believed in her and her mission of liberation. The English were struck into stupor. They remained motionless in their entrenchments whilst the Maid passed at the head of the relieving army. The inhabitants of Orleans, drunk with enthusiasm, and forgetting all their perils, rushed out from the walls and ran in crowds to meet her. According to an eyewitness: "They felt themselves to be comforted, and relieved by the Divine virtue which they had been told resided in this simple girl whom they all, men, women and children, looked upon with devout love."

The campaign of Jeanne on the Loire offers a spectacle which is unique in history. The Generals of Charles VII, Dunois, La hire, Gaucourt, and Xaintrailles marched against the enemy under the orders of a young girl of eighteen.

Difficulties without number arose in their path. A

circle of formidable forts had been built by the English around Orleans. Even a short delay would cause the surrender through famine of one of the greatest and strongest towns in the Kingdom. Before them were the best soldiers of England, commanded by their most famous generals, the very men who had beaten the French in a long series of victories.

Think, then, of the immense obstacles against which this young girl had to struggle. She had, it is true, brave men at her side, but they were demoralized by many defeats and were too badly organized to avoid new disasters.

The first attack, which was attempted in the absence of Jeanne, on the Fort of St. Loup was repulsed. Warned of impending defeat, the heroine sprang upon her horse, threw out her banner, reanimated the soldiers, and led them once more with reckless ardour to the attack.

"It was the first time," says Anatole France, in one of those rare passages in his book in which he does the Maid justice, "that Jeanne had seen a battle, and yet no sooner had she thrown herself into it, than she became the leader, because she was so by nature. She commanded better than the others, not because she knew more—as a fact, she knew less – but because she had the greater heart. When each thought of himself she alone thought of all. When each guarded himself she took no precaution whatever, having in advance given herself entirely to the cause. And yet this child who, like every other human being, feared suffering and death, and to whom her prophetic Voices had announced that she would be wounded, went straight forward and stood exposed on the edge of the moat, under the shower of crossbow-bolts and of bullets from the culverins, her Standard in her hand, rallying the combatants."

By this vigorous attack she broke the English line. One by one the forts were carried. In three days Orleans was delivered. Then fight followed fight like a series of lightning flashes in a thunderstorm. Every attack was a victory. First it was Jargeau, then Meung, then Beaugency. Finally, at Patay, the English were beaten in a pitched battle, and Talbot, their general, was made prisoner. Then came the march upon Reims, and Charles VII was consecrated King of France.

In two months Jeanne had repaired all recent disasters, had reconstituted, disciplined, and transformed the army, and had raised the courage of all.

"Before she came," said Dunois, "two hundred English could put to flight a thousand French, but with her to lead them a few hundred French could drive back an entire army."

In the "Mystère du Siége," a popular drama given for the first time in 1456 at Orleans, one of the actors declaims, "One of us is worth a hundred when we are under the banner of the Maid."

Certain authors, such as Thalamas, have tried to show that the situation at Orleans in 1429 was not really as serious as one generally supposes. The English were not numerous. The Burgundians had retired. The town was well provisioned, and could have resisted a long time. The people of Orleans were capable of delivering themselves by their own efforts.

Not only are all the historians, Michelet, Henri Martin, Wallon, Lavisse, etc., unanimous in stating that the situation was most dangerous for the besieged, but we may quote the opinion of another writer who cannot be suspected of partiality towards Jeanne. Anatole France writes:

"Tormented with doubts and fears, full of anxiety, without sleep, without rest, and with everything against them, the people of Orleans had begun to despair." On the other hand, the English were expecting reinforcements promised by the Regent. Five thousand fighting men had assembled at Paris under the orders of Sir John Fastolf to march to the help of the besiegers.

Finally, let us recall the evidence of the Duc D'Alençon during the Process of Rehabilitation. He spoke of the formidable forts which had been raised by the English.

"If I had been," said he, "in any one of them with a small garrison of men-at-arms I would have ventured to defy the power of a whole army, and I do not see how the attackers could have mastered my defence. I may add," said he, "that the captains who took part in these operations have declared to me that what occurred at Orleans was a miracle."

To these witnesses one may add the testimony of one of the besieged, Jean Luillier, a notable merchant of the city. He expressed himself thus: "I believe that if the Maid had not come to our aid we should very soon have been in the power of the besiegers. It was impossible that the people of Orleans could hold out longer against the power of adversaries who had so great a superiority."

Not less remarkable is the evidence which is written on a page of the register by a modest notary of the town, William Girault, and represents the feeling of all France of that day, "that this deliverance was the most obvious miracle which had ever been seen since the Passion of Christ."

The enthusiasm of the inhabitants was in proportions to the dangers which they had run. After the deliverance of their town the people of Orleans "offered to Jeanne, in return for what she had done, everything which they possessed in the world." So we are told in the Journal du Siége.

This part of the life of Jeanne is rich in prophecies which may add to those which have already been indicated. Her voices had told her that at her entrance into Orleans the English would not move. The facts confirmed this.

The barges which had to cross the river to embark the provisions could not do so, because the wind was unfavourable. Jeanne said, "Wait a little, and all will come into the town."

So it fell out, for the wind veered round and filled the sails.

She showed no anxiety on the subject of Marshal du Boussac, who had gone forward with a second convoy of provisions. She said, "I know well that no harm will befall him." The outcome exactly followed her prophecy.

Little by little, the increased confidence gained at Orleans spread over the whole of France. As the victories of Jeanne followed one another, the King announced them to all his loyal towns, inviting the population to praise God and to honour the Maid who "had always been present in person at the doings of France."

Everywhere the news was received and passed on with a delirious joy, while the people turned to the heroine with an ever-increasing devotion.

7

REIMS

THE prophecy of Jeanne concerning Orleans had been accomplished. There remained the march upon Reims and the consecration of Charles VII. Without losing an instant the Maid set to work to realize them. She quitted Orleans and went forth to find the Dauphin in the depths of Touraine. She finally rejoined him at Tours, and then followed him to Loches, pressing him continually to push on at once to bring this gallant enterprise to success. But this indolent, feeble prince hesitated between the ardour of the heroine and the misgivings of his cousellors, who considered it to be rash to risk a journey of sixty leagues across a country which bristled with fortresses and towns occupied by the enemy. To all their objection Jeanne made the same answer:

"I know it well, and I have considered all that. We shall succeed."

The enthusiasm of the people and of the Army was ever increasing. They clamoured to follow up the retreat of the English, who had evacuated the Loire and had fallen back upon Paris, abandoning their baggage and their artillery. Never had they received so rude a blow. Struck with terror they imagined that they saw in the air armies of phantoms advancing against them.

The rumour of these events re-echoed throughout France. Hope and energy began to re-awake. The general enthusiasm was such that Charles VII could no longer persist in his indifference. He piled honours upon the victorious Maid and her family, but he himself remained without enterprise and without courage. He did not even go to visit the people of Orleans. His principal counselors, La Trémoille and Regnault de Chartres, were uneasy and secretly annoyed at the success of Jeanne, which threw them into the shadow and made them jealous of the prestige which turned the thoughts and the hopes of all towards her. They asked themselves if their credit and their fortune were not about to be eclipsed in this great, irresistible, popular movement which had driven back the English invasion.

Finally, the public cry took a threatening tone, and it had to be obeyed. An army of 12.000 fighting men was gathered at Gien. Men of the nobler families mustered there from every part of France, and those who were too poor to equip themselves as knights begged to be allowed to serve as footmen. They set forth on the 29th June with little money, few provisions and an insufficient artillery.

On the 5th July they came before Troyes. The town, which was strongly fortified, well found in all things, and defended by an Anglo-Burgundian garrison, refused to open its gates. The French Army, with its meager resources, could not undertake a long siege. At the end of a few days the soldiers were reduced to gathering the herbs and the ripening crops which they found in the fields.

The King assembled his council to deliberate what course to follow. The Maid was not even called to it. The Chancellor laid before them the dangerous situation in which they found themselves and debated whether the Army should fall back, or continue its march on Reims. Each of the generals was asked to reply in turn.

~

Robert le Masson, Lord of Trèves-sur-Loire, remarked that the King having undertaken this expedition, not because it seemed easy, nor because he had a powerful army, nor the money needed for paying it, but entirely because Jeanne had said that it was the will of God and that they would meet with no resistance, they should, before going further, consult the Maid. This proposal was accepted. At that very moment, she, warned as to what was going on by her Voices, struck loudly on the door.

She entered and, addressing the King, she said:

"Gentle King of France, if you will deign to remain only two days in front of your town of Troyes, it will pay homage to you, either through fear of through love. Have no doubt about that."

The Chancellor replied: "If one were only sure of that, one might well wait six days for it."

"Have no doubt about it," said Jeanne once more.

She hurried through the camp to organize an instant attack, communicating to all the ardour with which she herself was burning. The night was spent in preparation. From the height of the walls and towers the besieged saw the French camp full of feverish activity. By the light of torches, knights, squires and soldiers were working hard to prepare the means for filling up the ditches, making fascines and ladders and building up screens for the artillery.

The spectacle was fantastic and impressive.

When the dawn whitened the horizon, the inhabitants of Troyes saw with terror that everything was ready for a furious assault. Columns of attack were drawn up at the most favourable points with their reserves behind them. The guns, well sheltered, were ready to open fire. The archers and the cross-bow men were ready in their places. The whole army, in silent ranks, awaited the signal. In front of them on the edge of the moat, her Standard in her hand, stood the Maid, surrounded by the trumpeters who should sound the assault.

The besieged, seized with panic, asked for terms. These were easily arranged. It was the obvious interest of the King to show mercy to those towns which were ready to surrender. The next day, 10th July, the English garrison marched out of the city, taking with them some French prisoners of war, whose freedom the King had forgotten to demand. These poor wretches, seeing Jeanne, threw themselves at her feet, imploring her help. She offered strong opposition to their departure, and the King was forced to pay their ransom.

Following the example of Troyes, Chalons and Reims opened their gates to Charles VII.

At Chalons, Jeanne had the joy of meeting several inhabitants of Domrémy who had come to see her again, and among them, Gerardin, a labourer, whose son, Nicholas, was her godson. She confided to them her thoughts and feelings, told them her hopes and fears, and recounted her battles and victories, the splendour of the coming consecration and the salvation of France, so lately sunk in despair.

Among these homely but honest folk, who brought back the atmosphere of her childhood, she felt at her ease. She told them that all these glories had left no mark at all upon her, and what a joy it would be to return to the village to renew her peaceable life in the midst of her family. But her mission held her near the King, and she had to submit to the will of those above her.

The struggle against the English gave her less trouble than the intrigues of the Court and the perfidy of the nobles.

"All I fear is treason," she said.

And as a fact it was by treason that she was destined to perish. In the case of every great missioner there is always some traitor hidden in the shadow who schemes his ruin.

Against the deep blue of the sky there stood out the high towers of the Cathedral of Reims, already many centuries old at the time of Jeanne d'Arc. Through the three open portals one could catch a glimpse of the vast aisles shining in the light of thousands candles where was gathered a strange mixed crowd of priests, lords, fighting men and citizens in holiday attire. The notes of the holy chants echoed amid the vaulted roofs, and from time to time warlike bugles broke in with their brazen cry.

The Guilds and the Corporations with their various ensigns displayed above them and all who could not find room in the Cathedral were assembled in the square outside. An immense mob of townspeople and villagers from the country around thronged round the edges of the great building, and could hardly be kept from breaking in by the steel-clad knights who were on guard, and by the archers who bore upon their jupons the Arms of France. Pages and squires held by the bridle the magnificent chargers of the King, the peers and the leaders of the Army. The people pointed out the black charger of the Maid which was held by one of her retainers.

Let us make our way under the high Gothic hall, and advance as far as the choir. The King, surrounded by twelve peers of the realm, lay and ecclesiastic, and by the Constable, Charles d'Albret, holding the State sword of France, was about to be made a knight. Near him, lower down, with her back against the right-hand pillar at a spot which they still point out, stood Jeanne, armed for war, her white Standard in her hand, that Standard which "after having been great in battle should be honoured in peace."

The King received the Holy Oil from the hands of the Archbishop of Reims, Regnault de Chartres. The latter took from the altar the crown, which was then held by the twelve peers, their hands spread out above the head of the Monarch. After having laid the crown upon him, Charles de Valois girded on the royal mantle, blue with scattered golden lilies. It was at this moment that the Maid, in a burst of emotion, threw herself at his feet, embracing his knees, and said to him:

"Gentle sire, thus is accomplished the Will of God, Who ordained that I should raise the siege of Orleans, and lead you to this city of Reims to receive your worthy Consecration, and so to prove that you are the true King and the heir to the Crown of France."

The trumpets broke out anew, the procession formed, and when in the opening of the great porch the King made his appearance, tremendous shouts of "Noel! Noel!" went up from the crowd on every side.

The pealing of the bugles vibrated through the high vaults. The chants and joyous cries swelled up into the heavens, and to their appeal thousands of invisible voices replied.

They were there, all the great spirits of Gaul, to celebrate the saving of their native country. They were there, all those who had loved and served to the death the noble land of France. They soared above the heads of the excited crowd. Here was Vercingetorix, followed by the heroes of Gergovie and of Alesia. Here were Clovis and his Franks. Here, too, Charles Martel and his companions, and Charlemagne, the great Emperor with the flowing beard. With his sword, called "Joyeuse," he saluted Jeanne and Charles VII. Then came Roland and his nobles, and the innumerable crowds of knights, priests, monks and soldiers, whose bodies repose under the heavy sepulchral stones, or are lost in the dust of the centuries. All those who had given their lives for France, they, too, were there and cried their Fatherland, and the awakening of Gaul.

The procession swept along through the narrow streets, and among the little squares. At the side of the King rode Jeanne, holding her banner, then came the Prince, the marshals and the captains, all richly clad and mounted on magnificent chargers. Pennons, flags and banderoles floated in the wind. But amidst these gaily-dressed lords, and warriors in their shining armour, all eyes were fixed on the young girl who had brought them to the city of Consecration, even as she predicted in her village at a time when she was the simple peasant, the little unknown shepherdess.

The whole town was en fête. People had come from afar for the Consecration. Jacques d'Arc, the father of Jeanne, had arrived two days before from Domrémy, together with Durand Lexart.

They put up at the inn of the Ane Rayé in the Rue du Parvis. It was a moving scene when the heroine, accompanied by her brother Pierre, saw once again her aged father. She threw herself on her knees and implored his pardon for having left him without his assent, adding that it was the will of God.

At the request of the Maid the King gave them audience, and granted to the inhabitants of the villages of Greux and Domrémy exemption from all taxes. The expenses of Jacques d'Arc were paid from the public funds, and a horse was given him, at the charge of the town, to return to his own home.

Jeanne showed herself in the streets, receiving with modesty and with kindness the humble suppliants who came to her. The people pressed around her. All wished to touch her hands and her ring. There was not one who was not convinced that she had been sent by God to bring to an end the calamities which oppressed the Kingdom. All this happened on Sunday, 17th July, 1429, a date which marked the culminating point of the career of Jeanne d'Arc.

None the less, Michelet is wrong in saying that her mission should have ended at Reims, and that she disobeyed the Voices in continuing the struggle.

This assertion is denied by the words of the heroine herself in her declarations to the examiners of Poitiers and to the judges at Reims. Above all, she asserts it in her letter sent to the English captains before Orleans under the date of the 22nd March.

"Whenever I find your people in France I will drive them out, whether they will or not. I have been sent by God to rid France of you entirely."

There can, then, be no doubt about it. The idea that the mission of Jeanne came to an end at Reims was only put forward at the time of the Process of Rehabilitation to conceal from posterity the disloyalty, or rather one might say, the crime of Charles VII and his counselors and so to free them from the heavy responsibility which weighs upon them.

It is with this objection that history has been falsified and mutilated by them. The evidence of witnesses has been altered, the record of the questions asked at Poitiers has been destroyed, and thus an odious act—a work of falsehood and iniquity—has been accomplished.

None the less, it was not without apprehension and not without regrets that Jeanne went on with her arduous mission. Some days later, riding between Dunois and the Chancellor, Regnault de Chartres, she said, "How I wish that it would please God that I might now return, leaving these arms, and that I might go to serve my father and mother, and to care for the flocks with my sister and brothers, who would be right glad to see me once more."

These words show that all the glory of her triumph and the splendours of the Court had never dazzled her. She had come to the height of her glory. The adoration of a whole people mounted up to her. It is no exaggeration to say that she was the first in the Kingdom and that her prestige eclipsed that of the King. Yet she only longed for the peace of the fields and the simple pleasures of her home. Neither her victories nor the power which she had gained had changed her. She remained simple and modest in the midst of her greatness. What a lesson for those who are unbalanced by the least success and turn giddy if any favour of fortune comes their way!

8

COMPIÈGNE

"To Paris!" cried the Maid, the day after the Consecration.

"To Paris!" cried all the army.

If they had marched straight on to the capital as Jeanne desired, there was every chance that they might have captured it on account of the confusion which reigned amount the English. Charles VII lost precious time, and the Duke of Bedford profited by it in order to reinforce Paris. He summoned from England a fresh army to help him, raised by the Cardinal of Winchester, uncle of King Henry, and intended originally to fight against the Hussites.

From this moment the star of Jeanne began to wane. After the triumphs and the dazzling victories there came the dark hours, the hours of trial working up towards prison and martyrdom. As the fame of the heroine spread, and as her glory surpassed all other glories, hatred too increased around her. Intrigues broke out among these great lords whose plans she had thwarted, and whose dark conspiracies she had unveiled. All the perfidious courtiers whom she had eclipsed, as well as the men of the Church with hearts full of guile, who could not pardon her for saying that she was sent without their authority straight from Heaven, and that she preferred the inspiration of her Voices to any advice from them, plotted against her. Then also there were many of the warlike chiefs who had been beaten in a hundred fights, and who saw themselves suddenly surpassed in military science by a girl from the fields —these men, hurt in their pride, had sworn her ruin. They awaited the favourable moment, and that moment was at hand.

The English had been prostrated by their defeat. Their principal army was destroyed, their best captains were dead or prisoners, their soldiers deserted out of fear of the Maid. They no longer doubted the supernatural power of her whom they called "the Sorceress of France." If Charles VII, immediately after his Oath, had hastened to Paris, the great town would have given itself up without a battle.

Six weeks were lost in hesitation. Then, when at last they arrived before the capital, no precaution had been taken. The orders of Jeanne had not been executed. The moats had not been filled up. The attack was not hard-pushed. They had given her as lieutenants the two warlike chiefs who were most hostile to her, "and the two most ferocious men who ever lived," said Michelet—Raoul de Gaucourt and Marshal de Retz, the odious magician, destined later to mount the scaffold for the crime of sorcery. The King refused to be present. In vain they sent message after message to him. He would not come. The Duc d'Alençon hurried to find him at Senlis. He promised to come, and broke his word.

At the attack of the St. Honoré Gate, Jeanne, as

usual, showed herself to be heroic. During the whole day she kept her place on the edge of the ditch under a reign of missiles, exhorting the soldiers as they attacked. At sunset she was deeply wounded by a crossbow arrow in the thigh, and lay stretched on the turf. She did not cease to urge on the soldiers, crying from time to time: "The King! The King! Let the King show himself!" But the King did not come.

Towards eleven o'clock in the evening several of the leaders seized her and dragged her away against her will. They retreated to St. Denis, where the King was taking measures to regain the castles of the Loire. Jeanne could not bring herself to lose sight of the spires of Paris.

"She was, as it were, chained before the great city by some force beyond herself."

Next morning she wished to recommence the attack. But they could no longer advance. By order of the King the bridges had been cut and retreat imposed upon them.

Thus ended one of the great infamies of history. The very people to whom God had sent a saving Messiah had intrigued against her. They had succeeded in ruining the mission of Jeanne d'Arc, and according to the strong expression of Henri Martin "had made the Almighty a Liar." Their selfishness and blindness were such that the action of Providence was suspended, because they were unworthy of it.

After the check at Paris Jeanne endured a long period of uncertainty, trouble, and internal dissension. For eight months she experienced alternately successes and reverses, success at St. Pierre Lamontier, reverse at La Charité. She felt that the fortune had abandoned her. At the moat of Melun her Voices said to her:

"Jeanne, you will be taken prisoner before the Feast of St. John."

This change of fortune must be entirely attributed to the ill-will of mankind, and to the ingratitude of the King and his counselors, which threw a thousand obstacles in her way, and caused all her enterprises to miscarry.

Was she weakened thereby? In no wise. It is from this moment that she became truly great, greater even than her victories had made her. Her trials, her captivity and her martyrdom, so nobly borne, lift her high above the most illustrious conquerors, and make her sublime in the eyes of posterity.

In the depths of her prison, before the Tribunal of Rouen, and even on the scaffold she appears to us more imposing than in the turmoil of battle or in the frenzy of triumph. Her bearing, her sufferings, her inspired words, her tears and her long-drawn agony from one of the purest glories of France, an object of admiration for all centuries and of emulation for all nations!

Adversity adorned her with a holy aureole. By her heroic acceptance of ill-fortune, by the greatness of her soul, in reverses and in the face of death, she has become a just cause of pride for the women of France and an object of veneration for all those in whose hearts the feeling of moral beauty and love of country vibrates. The glory of arms is fine, but it is only genius, sanctity and suffering which have a right to the full apotheosis of history.

~

The siege of La Charité having failed, Jeanne was recalled to the Court, but soon inaction fretted her and once again her ardour reasserted itself. She abandoned the King to his pleasure and his feasts, and at the head of a devoted troop she threw herself into Compiègne, which was besieged. It was there that during a sortie the Governor of the town, William de Flavy, dropped the drawbridge behind her, so that she was unable to re-enter the place, and was taken prisoner by the Count of Luxembourg, who belonged to the party of Burgundy.

What responsibility shall we ascribe to the Lord of Flavy in this incident? Some have seen premeditated treason. The chancellor, Regnault de Chartres, had visited Compiègne a little time before, and had had interviews with the Duke of Burgundy. The greater number of historians, however—Martin, Quicherat, Wallon and Anatole France, believe in the good faith of this captain.

In spite of their arguments, the part which he played has remained somewhat equivocal and ill-defined. It is true that the recent historian M. Pierre Champion, who has written about De Flavy, has not been able to draw any definite conclusion from an examination of the documents, and has not discovered any actual proof against the man. According to the psychic information which I have received, there is no reason to believe that there was premeditation, but rather that he took advantage of a situation which happened to offer itself in order to get rid of a person who had become a stumbling-block for certain ambitions.

If there was no premeditated plot against Jeanne, there was, none the less, treason in the matter, inasmuch as De Flavy made no attempt to rescue her. Surrounded by the Burgundians in the angle of the causeway between Margny and the fortification which defended the head of the bridge, only a few yards from the Sally Port, she might easily have been rescued. At that critical moment, the Captain of Compiègne was close up with several hundred men, and saw all that passed. He made no effort and abandoned Jeanne to her destiny. It is in this that the treason appears flagrant.

Jeanne was first confined in the Castle of Beaulieu, some distance from Compiègne, and was then transferred to the dungeon of Beau Revoir belonging to the Count of Luxembourg. Taken from one prison to another, from Arras to Drugy and thence to Crotoy, it was not until 21st November, after a pressing summons and threats from the University of Paris, that she was sold to the English, her bitter enemies, for ten thousand pounds, and in addition a donation for the soldier who had actually captured her.

Jeanne of Luxembourg was of high degree, but of a narrow spirit and of decayed fortunes. He had inscribed upon his banner a depressing motto:

"One cannot attempt the impossible."

How infinitely more vibrant was the cry of his contemporary, Jacques Coeur: "To the valiant heart nothing is impossible."

Deep in debt and almost ruined, Luxembourg could not resign himself to adversity, nor in consequence could he refuse the £10,000 which the King of England offered. At that price he sold Jeanne and handed her over. £10,000 in gold! It was an enormous sum for those days. The English were at the end of their resources, and could no longer pay their own officials. For want of money the sittings of the Court of Justice were suspended at Paris for many weeks. The scrivener who wrote the Acts of Parliament had his work interrupted because he could not buy parchment, but when it came to a question of buying Jeanne, the English never hesitated to find this large sum. How did they get it? In a very familiar fashion. They laid a heavy tax on the whole of Normandy, which brings to light a singular fact that it was French money that paid for the blood of Jeanne d'Arc.

∼

In the depths of her prison Jeanne's chief trouble was not about her own lot, but rather, as she sadly expressed it, because "I can no longer serve the noble country of France." On hearing the news that the good people of Compiègne were threatened with death if the town were taken, she hurled herself down from the Tower of Beau Revoir in the hope of rejoining them.

"I had heard," she explained to her judges, "that people of Compiègne down to the age of seven years were to be put to fire and sword, and I would rather risk death for myself than continue to live after such a fate had befallen these good people."

Stage by stage, from dungeon to dungeon, she was brought at last to Crotoy on the borders of that part of Normandy which was occupied by the English. They shut her up in one of the guardian towers which flank the estuary of the Somme. From her barred windows her view stretched over a panorama of sand-hills, beyond which lay the immensity of the sea. It was the first time that she had ever contemplated that wonderful spectacle and it impressed her profoundly.

The sea with its foaming waves, its limitless horizon, and the constant changes reflected from its surface! She, so sensitive to the harmonies of Heaven and earth, to the sun by day and to the stars by night, lost herself in the contemplation of that vast expanse, sometimes silver grey, sometimes deeply blue, glimmering at night with the glitter of the stars. She listened with surprise to the vague murmurings of the sea. When at the hour of high tide the sob of the falling billows came to her ears an immense feeling of sadness fell upon her. The English were coming, the English who had bought her so dear. Since she left Compiègne she had been the prisoner of the Burgundians, men of the same race and language as herself, who had used her with some consideration. But now, what could she hope from these fierce foreigners who she had beaten so many times, and who, with their furious hatred towards her, would never miss a chance of injuring her. A terrible agony tore her soul and she prayed. But the Voices again and again replied,

"Take everything in good part."

She had to wait thus at Crotoy for three weeks. One day the ladies of Abbeville came to visit her, to console her, and their tears for an hour or two were mixed with her own.

9

ROUEN—THE PRISON

JEANNE was now in the hands of the English. They gagged her that she might not communicate with the people, and conducted her under a strong escort to the Castle of Rouen. There she was thrown into a dungeon, and shut in an iron cage.

"They made for me," she tells us, "a sort of cage into which they put me. I was closely confined in it. I had one strong chain round my neck, another round my waist and others at my hands and feet. I should have succumbed in this dreadful position, if God and my guardian spirits had not upheld me by their consolations. Nothing can describe the touching care and the loving help which they gave me. Dying of hunger, half-clad, surrounded by discomfort and weighed down by my irons, I yet found in my faith sufficient strength to pardon those who tortured me."

It was atrocious treatment. Jeanne was a prisoner of war. She was a woman and yet they shut her up like a savage beast in an iron cage. A little later, however, the English contented themselves by tying her to a great beam with two chains attached to her ankles.

Thus began an agony of six months, an agony without example in history, an agony more painful even than that of Christ, for Christ at least was a man, and here we have to do with a young girl of nineteen at the mercy of brutal, stupid and sensual ruffians. Five soldiers, rascally fellows, the dregs of the English Army, according to the historians, kept guard day and night in her prison. Imagine what a young woman in chains might expect from vile and ruffianly men, drunk with fury against her who they looked upon as the cause of all their defeats. These wretches overwhelmed her with ill-treatment. Often they tried to do her a violence and beat her brutally. She complained of her treatment to her judges in the course of the trial, and many times when they made their way into her prison to interrogate her, they found her in tears with her face swollen and bruised by the blows which she had received.

Think of the horrors of her situation—of her thoughts and fears as a woman—exposed to every sort of outrage. Think of the continual want of repose and the broken sleep which weakened her bodily powers and sapped her energy in the midst of these insistent anxieties and pains. Alone among these wretches she naturally did not wish to cease to wear her male clothing, and they reproached her for this act of modesty as if it were a crime. Her visitors were no less abominable than her jailors. The Count of Luxembourg who had sold her came one day to mock at her in her dungeon. He was accompanied by the Counts of Warwick and Stafford, together with the Bishop of Thérouanne, Chancellor of the King of England.

"I have come to rescue you," said he, "on condition

that you will promise me never to bear arms against us again."

"You are mocking me," she cried. "I know well that you have neither the will nor the power to do this." And as he insisted, she continued, "I know well that the English will put me to death, believing that after my death they can win the Kingdom of France. But if there were a hundred thousand more of them than there are, still they should not have this Kingdom."

These words made them furious. Lord Stafford drew his dagger to strike Jeanne, but Lord Warwick held him back from her.

Then there were her judges who ordered an unworthy priest, a traitor and a spy, Loyceleur, to introduce himself into her prison dressed as a layman. Pretending that he was a native of Lorraine and a prisoner of the English, he gained the confidence of Jeanne and got her to confess to him. During their interviews concealed notaries listened through an opening made for the purpose, and wrote down the confidential utterances of the heroine.

Who would say what she suffered in the darkness of her soul? Abandoned by all, betrayed and sold, she touched the very limits of misery.

She learned to know those hours of agony, of moral torture, when everything grows dark around us, and the Voices of Heaven seem to be silenced; when the Invisible loses touch with us, while, at the same time, all terrestrial furies and hatred are simultaneously loosened and poured down upon us. All great missioners have endured these grievous hours, and she underwent more than all, this poor child exposed without protection to the most vile outrages. Why does God permit such things? It is in order to rest the soul and the heart of the faithful, to try their faith in Him, and finally, it is that their merits may ever increase, and that the crown which He reserves for them may gain in splendour and in beauty.

But, one may ask, how could Jeanne, weak and bound, escape the infamous advances of her visitors and of her guardians? How could she preserve her purity and her sanctity in such terrible conditions?

Well, in those terrible hours, more dreadful for her than death itself, the Invisible intervened. In the cold dark prison a radiant troop glimmered up. Beings whom she only could see, and whom she called "her Brothers of Paradise," hastened to help her, to sustain her, and to give her the strength to hold out against the dangers which threatened her.

These spirits comforted her, saying to her ever, "To suffer is to grow greater, to grow higher."

In the midst of all the shadows which enfolded her, a ray of hope always shone. Sweet chants came to her ears like some echo from the harmonies of space. Her Voices consoled her and kept on saying to her, "Take courage, you will be delivered by a glorious victory." In her simple faith she believed that this deliverance would be earthly liberty. Alas! It was the deliverance of death, the death by martyrdom, described as victory even as our ancestors, the Druids, used to name it. It needed only that to give to this saintly figure its whole sublime radiance.

Is it not the privilege of great souls to be destined to suffer for a noble cause? Must they not pass through the crucible of trial in order to show all the virtues, all the treasures, all the splendours which are in them? A great death is the necessary crown of a great life, a life of devotion and of sacrifice. It is the initiation into a higher existence. But in these hours of sadness, in this final purification, such souls are upheld by a superhuman strength, a strength which enables them to face all and to conquer all.

10

ROUEN — THE TRIAL

WE now come to the trial. During all the period covered by this hard and terrible captivity, Jeanne had to undergo the long and tortuous phases of a trial, the like of which has never been seen before in the world.

Against her was all that the spirit of evil could suggest—wicked hypocrisy, cunning, perfidy and servile ambition. There were seventy-one priests and doctors, hard-hearted Pharisees to a man, all of them nominally men of the Church, but men for whom religion is only a mask covering their ardent passions, their cupidity, their spirit of intrigue and their narrow fanaticism.

On the other side, alone, without support, without counsel, without defender, is a girl nineteen years of age, innocence and purity incarnate, her heroic soul in a virginal body, with a sublime and tender heart ready to make any sacrifice to save her country, to fulfill her mission with fidelity and to give an example of virtue and of duty.

Never has human nature risen higher on the one side, or fallen lower on the other.

History has allotted the responsibility. I have no desire now to say anything which may re-awaken political or religious hatreds. Is not the name of Jeanne d'Arc, amid all glorious names, that which can rally round it common sentiments of admiration, to whatever party we may belong?

The Church has tried to clear itself from the accusation which has weighed heavily upon it during all these centuries. To this end it has endeavoured to throw the whole odium of the condemnation of Jeanne upon Pierre Cauchon, Bishop of Beauvais. It has disowned him and covered him with its maledictions, but is Cauchon really the only great culprit?

Let us recall one incident. On the 26th May, 1430, three days after the capture of Jeanne before Compiègne, the Vicar-General of the Grand Inquisition of France, sitting at Paris, wrote to the Duke of Burgundy to beg him and to "order him under pain of the Law to send to him as a prisoner a certain woman named Jeanne—a maid strongly suspected of crimes tainted with heresy, that she may appear before the Controller of the Holy Inquisition."

Thus, this redoubtable Tribunal of the Holy office, which had become a mere phantom at this period, reappeared and stole out from the shadow in order to claim the greatest victim that had ever appeared before it, and the University of Paris, the principal ecclesiastical body in France, supported its pretensions.

Anatole France, who is well-informed on this point, tell us:

"In their fear of the Maid it was not merely a Bishop who got the Holy Inquisition to move in the matter, it was the daughter of Kings, the Mother of

Learning, the beautiful clear sun of France and of Christianity – the University of Paris. It claimed for itself the privilege of looking into all cases which dealt with heresy, and its opinion, which was asked from all parts, carried authority over the whole face of the globe wherever the Cross was planted."

For a year it kept on demanding that the Maid should be handed over to the Inquisition as being one who was suspected of sorcery. The same author tells us later:

"After having taken counsel with the doctors and masters of the University of Paris, the Bishop of Beauvais presented himself on the 14th July at the campo Compiègne, and claimed the Maid as belonging to his Department of Justice."

In support of his demand he produced letters addressed by the University to the Duke of Burgundy and to the Lord of Luxembourg. It was the second time that the University had claimed Jeanne from the Duke.

It feared that others might set her free in some indirect way, and that so she might escape for ever from its power. At the same time its messenger was charged to offer money in exchange for the captive.

Pierre Cauchon, Bishop of Beauvais, who had been chased out of his See by the people because he had taken the side of the English, had thoroughly mastered the case and directed the whole trial.

It is incontestable that he played the most important part in it, but the Deputy Inquisitor, Jean Lemaitre, checked all his decisions regarding the composition of the Tribunal, on which on several occasions he himself sat. When the Bishop of Beauvais was unable to do it, Jean Lemaitre in person presided. That has been established by all the documents.

The Deputy Inquisitor signed and certified as authentic the reports of the sittings. These were drawn up in duplicate by the clerks of the Tribunal. There is one copy in the library of the Chamber of Deputies, and it is sealed with the seal of the Inquisition.

In trials for heresy it was the law that all decisions and judgments should be given by two judges, the Bishop and the Inquisitor. That is exactly what occurred at Rouen as elsewhere. It is impossible, therefore, to get away from the fact that Cauchon was supported by the Inquisitorial Tribunal.

But this is not all. The Bishops of Coutances and of Lisieux were consulted in the course of the trial, and they approved of the accusation. It is worth recording that the Bishop of Lisieux, Zenon de Castiglione, voted for the condemnation of Jeanne, giving as his reason that she was of too lowly a condition to be inspired by God. One may well ask oneself what the Apostles of Jesus, those humble workmen or boatmen of Galilee, or what Jesus Himself, the son of a carpenter, would have thought of this reply.

The Bishops of Thérouanne, of Noyon, and of Norwich also took part in the trial, and all three joined in the cross-examination of the Maid.

Cauchon surrounded himself with persons of importance and theologians of note. He had sitting on the Tribunal Thomas de Courcelles, whom later they called "the light of the Council of Bale and the second Gerson," Pierre Maurice and Jean Beaupère, both of whom had been lecturers of the University of Paris. Also he had doctors and masters of theology, such as William Erard, Nicole Midi, Jacques de Touraine and a number of Abbots with their crosiers and their mitres from the great abbeys of Normandy.

Of all these eminent clerics not one showed himself to be impartial. To a man they were partisans of the English and enemies of Jeanne.

The Prosecutor, Jean d'Estivet the agent of Cauchon, a man without honour or scruples, was particularly forward in his expressions of hatred and in his violence towards the accused. No attention was paid to the legitimate demand of Jeanne that they ought to introduce into the Tribunal an equal number of clerics belonging to the French party. She appealed also to the Pope and to the Council. It was in vain.

All the judges, assessors, canons and doctors of authority received from the English for each sitting a fee which was equivalent to 40 francs of our actual money. The receipts for this are found in the account of the trial. There were nearly a hundred assessors, but they did not all sit at the same time. Those who were most hostile to Jeanne received additional presents.

The King of England gave to the various members of the Tribunal guarantees in case "those who were in favour of the errors of Jeanne should endeavour to drag them before the Pope, the Council, or any other body."

There had been many consultations at the Sorbonne, among others that of the 19th April, which was confirmed by the four Faculties on the 14th May. All of them summed up against the Maid.

One should add that the Inquisitor-General, Jean Graverend, preached a sermon in the Church of St. Martin-in-the-Fields after the punishment of Jeanne, in which he repeated all the terms of the accusation and approved of the sentence. Shortly afterwards the Church named Pierre Cauchon as successor to the episcopal See of Lisieux. If at a later date he was excommunicated it was not in punishment of his crime, but simply because he refused to give up a right which was claimed by the Vatican. It was on a question of money that this prelate was threatened with the pontifical thunderbolt, which never for one moment menaced him during that long period when he had been the guilty wretch who had brought about the condemnation of the liberator of his own country.

As a fact, there was not one voice raised in the whole of Christendom to protest against the iniquitous judgment of which Jeanne was the victim. She had no support either from those clergy who had remained French, or from those clergy who had gone over to the English. On the contrary, a circular form Regnault de Chartres, Archbishop of Reims, to his subordinates, shows us the shameful state of mind of Charles VII and his counsellors.

There has been discovered, in a document attached to the Charter of the Hôtel de Ville of Reims, the analysis of a message sent by the Chancellor to the inhabitants of the chief town of his bishopric, conceived in the following terms:

He tells them of the capture of Jeanne before Compiègne, and "that she would not take advice, and that she did everything according to her own will. God, therefore, had allowed Jeanne, the maid, to be taken because she had been puffed up with pride and had dressed herself in rich garments and had not tried to do that which God had commanded, but had followed her own will."

Meanwhile, Charles VII, surrounded as he was by evil counsellors, had, none the less, been the object of high and pressing solicitations in favour of the heroine.

Jacques Gelu, Archbishop of Embrun, his ancient teacher, wrote to his royal pupil after the capture of Jeanne venturing to remind him of all that the Maid had done for the Crown of France. He prayed him to examine his own conscience thoroughly and to make sure "if there were not offences towards God which had brought about this misfortune. I recommend you," he added, "to get back this girl. To save her life, spare neither means nor money nor any conceivable effort unless you are ready to face unbelievable disgrace and the reproach of dire ingratitude."

He counselled him to order that prayers should be put up everywhere for the delivery of Jeanne that she might obtain pardon from whatever Tribunal should judge her.

Thus spoke this aged Bishop who had been the counsellor of the Dauphin during the dark days, and who dearly loved both the king and the kingdom.

They could easily have ransomed Jeanne from the Lord of Luxembourg. They took no steps to do so. They could even have carried her off by a sudden attack. The French occupied Louviers, only a short distance from Rouen. They remained motionless. Those who before the journey to Reims spoke of attacking Normandy were now silent.

At the least they could have taken legal steps to counteract the sentence of the Tribunal by bringing influence to bear which the judges would have respected. The Bishop of Beauvais, who conducted the trial, was a subordinate of the Archbishop of Reims. The latter could insist that he should at least give him a complete account of every sitting. He abstained from all intervention.

They could also have supported the protests of the family of Jeanne. They could have claimed an appeal to the Pope or to the Council. They could have threatened the English with reprisals on Talbot and the other prisoners or war in order to save the life of the Maid. Nothing was done.

"It is certain," says Wallon, "that Jeanne was left to her fate. Her death entered into the calculations of those wretched, avaricious men, Regnault de Chartres, La Trémoille, and all the other debased characters, who desired to keep their ascendancy in the counsels of the King, and therefore, sacrificed not only Jeanne, but their Prince, their Fatherland, and God Himself."

When we weigh everything, the responsibility for the punishment and death of Jeanne seems to us to fall in an equal degree upon the Church and upon the two crowns of England and of France.

As regards the Church there is one thing which should be remembered. It is that if so many prelates and priests, and even the Inquisition itself, were concerned in the Process of Condemnation of Jeanne, it was also at the direction of the Grande Inquisitor, Jean Brehal, that the Process of Rehabilitation was brought about. If priests were found to condemn the Maid, there were others as numerous who were found to glorify her, among them the great Gerson and the Archbishop of Embrum.

It is clear that Jeanne having been burnt as a sorceress, the Crown of France could not and would not remain under the suspicion of having had diabolical dealings. To bring about the Process of Revision which should clear the matter up, it was necessary for three long years to negotiate with the Court of Rome. All the influence of the King and of his Councils was needed, an influence which must have weighed very heavily with the Roman Pontiff at this time of schism, since three different popes were simultaneously disputing authority over the Christian world. It needed, therefore, powerful pressure to bring about this revision, and without this pressure and this constant insistence, it is probable that there never would have been reparation.

"The Tribunal of Rehabilitation," says Joseph Fabre, "after waiting twenty-five years, granted impunity to the executioners, even while it proclaimed the innocence of the sufferer. Furthermore, although it declared Jeanne clear from the crime of heresy, it admitted that if she had been a heretic she would have deserved the stake, and thus it upheld the decision of the original judges so far as it involved this wicked principle of intolerance of which she had been the victim."

But however tardy and incomplete, let us accept this reparation for what it is worth. Let us remember, too, that processions of expiation were organized in the chief towns of France, and that the clergy took a large part in them. Let us remember, also, that at a later date the English themselves glorified the memory of Jeanne. One of their poets, Southey, proclaimed her to be the greatest heroine of the human race. Many voices were raised in England to demand that some sort of reparation should be made in the public places of Rouen by representatives of the Crown and of Parliament.

Let us bear all this in mind and recognize that before the great figure of Jeanne all resentment must disappear, all hatred must vanish. It is not over her august name that a quarrel of parties or nations should spring up. For if this name is a symbol of patriotism with us, it is also, above all, a symbol of universal peace and conciliation.

Jeanne belongs to all, though most of all to France. And yet if an exception should be made within our own nation in favour of any group or cult, if it is conceivable that Jeanne should belong to some of us rather than to others, inflexible logic would point out that it is to those who have known how to understand her life, to penetrate its mystery, and who even to-day try to learn by the study of the Invisible world those forces and those aids which have assured her triumph, and which they still desire to use for the moral good and the salvation of their country.

Let us return to the judges at Rouen. When one studies the various phases of the trial it becomes clear that in the minds of these sophists with their frozen hearts, and in the thoughts of theologians already sold to England, Jeanne had been condemned in advance. Had they not all seen with rage and envy a woman raised up in the name of the God whose representatives they claimed to be, yet pleading the cause which they, believing it to be lost, had betrayed—the cause of France? All these men had only one object, one desire —it was to revenge on this woman their threatened authority and their compromised dignity. By them, as by the English, Jeanne was pre-destined for death, but then death alone would not suffice for their political views nor for their hatred. They wished that she should be dishonoured by denying her own mission, and that her dishounor be reflected back upon the King and upon all France.

To bring this about there was but one way—to obtain from her a recantation, a disavowal of her own claims. It was necessary to make her admit that her inspiration came from the devil. A trial for sorcery might lead to this. To this end they would use every possible means – cunning, spying, ill-treatment, all the sufferings and all the horrors of the hideous prison in which the purity of Jeanne was for ever exposed to danger. Threats and even torture were resorted to. But Jeanne resisted everything.

Picture to yourself this vaulted hall into which there filters a dim light through the narrow openings. One might describe it as a funeral crypt. The Tribunal has assembled. Sixty judges are sitting there under the presidency of the Bishop of Beauvais, to whom the English had promised the Archbishopric of Rouen if he would but serve their interests. Above them, a bitter irony, the image of the crucified Christ is displayed upon the wall. Then at the end of the hall and at every door one sees the glitter of the weapons of the stern-faced English soldiers.

Why this display of force? All to judge a girl nineteen years of age!

Jeanne is very pale, drooping, loaded with chains. She is weakened by the suffering of her long captivity. She is there alone in the midst of her enemies who have sworn her destruction. Alone? Oh, no! For if men abandon her, if her King forgets her, if the nobles of France make no attempt to save her from the English either by force or by ransom, at least there are invisible beings who watch over her, uphold her and inspire her to such replies as sometimes silence her own judges.

And what a turmoil! What a tumult! In their fury and excitement the judges argue and quarrel among themselves. Questions shower down upon her. They use all their ingenuity to entrap her by hypocritical pretexts or to worry her by questions so subtle and so difficult that, according to the expression of one of the assessors, Isambard de la Pierre, "the greatest clerics in the world would have found a great deal of difficulty in answering them."

And yet she answered. Sometimes with an admirable wit—sometimes with a good sense so profound, and with words so sublime, that none could doubt that she was inspired by higher forces. Chill fear fell upon those present when she would say in speaking of them: "They are there although you cannot see them." But all these men were too deeply involved in their crime to weaken.

Thus they tried to overwhelm Jeanne physically and morally. They made her undergo interrogation after interrogation, sometimes two a day, of a duration of three hours each, and during all that time they compelled her to remain standing, charged with her heavy chains.

But Jeanne did not allow herself to weaken. This sinister place was in her eyes a new field of battle. There she showed her grand soul, her masculine courage. The invisible power which inspired her broke out into vehement words which sometimes terrified her accusers.

She addressed the Bishop of Beauvais:

"You say that you are my judge. I am not sure of that, but beware that you do not judge me falsely, for if you do you will put yourself in great danger. I warn you so that when the Lord chastises you I will feel that I have done my duty in telling you. I have come from God. I have nothing to do here. Leave me to the judgment of that God from Whom I have come."

They asked her this perfidious question:

"Do you believe that you are in the Grace of God?"

"If I am not I trust He will place me there, and if I am that He will hold me there."

"You think, then, that it is useless to go to confession, although in a state of mortal sin?"

"I have never committed a mortal sin. My Voices would have reproached me for it. My spirits would have deserted me."

"What do your Voices tell you?"

"They tell me, 'Fear nothing, answer bravely. God will help you.'"

They tried to convict her of magic and of sorcery, pretending that she had made use of different objects which had a mysterious power.

"Is it your standard that supports you, or is it you who support the standard?"

She replied, "Whether the victory came from the standard of from Jeanne, it was all from God."

"But the hope of having this victory, was it founded on your standard or on yourself?"

"On God and on nothing else."

How many others in her place would have resisted the temptation of claiming the merit of her victories? Pride may be found even in the most noble and the most pure souls. Nearly all of us are inclined to place a value upon our own acts, to exaggerate their importance and to glorify ourselves above reason. And yet, all comes to us from God. Without Him we should be nothing, we could do nothing. Jeanne knew it, and amid the atmosphere of glory which surrounded her, she remained humble, attributing to God alone the merit of the work done. Far from becoming vain over her mission, she brought it down to its real proportions, claiming that she had only been an instrument in the service of the Supreme Power.

"It has pleased God to act thus by the strength of a simple maid in order to repel the enemies of the King."

But how admirable an instrument! Full of wisdom, intelligence and virtue! What profound submission to the will of the Higher!

"All my deeds and my words are from the hands of God, and my thoughts turn only to Him."

∽

One day the Bishop of Beauvais penetrated into the dungeon. He was clad in his sacerdotal robes and seven priests accompanied him.

Jeanne had been warned by her Voices. She knew that this interview was to be decisive.

Her voices had told her to resist bravely, to defend the truth, and to despise death. Therefore, at the sight of the priests her wary body was drawn erect. Her features became animated and her eyes reflected her strong resolution.

"Jeanne," said the Bishop, "are you willing to submit to the Church?"

A terrible question in the middle ages, and on it depended the lot of the heroine.

"I refer all things to God, and God has always inspired me."

"This is a grave saying. Between you and God there stands the Church. Are you willing—yes or no—to submit yourself to the Church?"

"I came to the King for the safety of France, and was sent by God and His Holy Spirits—to that Church, the Church of the beyond, I submit in everything which I have said and done."

"So you refuse to submit to the Church? You refuse to give up your diabolical visions?"

"I answer to God alone. As to my visions, I do not accept the judgment of any man."

This was the turning-point of the trial.

They desired to know above all things if Jeanne would prefer the authority of her revelations over the orders of the Church. At the time of the Process of Rehabilitation both judges and witnesses had but one desire, which was to show that Jeanne had hesitated and had then accepted the authority of the Pope and of the Church. Even to-day this is the argument of those who introduce the heroine into the Catholic Paradise. But in her trial Jeanne in all her replies remained resolute. Her thought was clear, her words determined.

She had a profound realization of the point which she was defending. In truth this solemn debate was carried on between two inflexible principles. On the one side was the law, the traditional authority, which supposes the infallibility of a power which had endured for so many centuries. On the other side stood inspiration and the sacred rights of the individual conscience. Inspiration showed itself there in the most convincing, the most touching form that one has seen in all the centuries.

One must understand, then, that the Interrogatories of Rouen, more even than the Process of Rehabilitation, show us Jeanne in all her grandeur, in all the splendour of her passionate replies, replies where her voice vibrated and where her glance, as a witness said, "shot out lightnings."

Even her judges were fascinated. Never at any time had she shown herself more beautiful and more imposing.

"I answer to God alone," she said.

At last, faced by this resolution, by this will which nothing could bend, they hesitated no longer.

On the 9th of May, Jeanne was led into the torture chamber. The torturers were there with their sinister implements, which were prepared and heated in the fire. Jeanne stood firm. She spoke in defence of France and the ungrateful King who had abandoned her.

"If you tear me limb from limb," said she, "and my soul from my body, I can say nothing else."

She was not handed over to the torturers, not from any sentiment of pity or humanity, but because in her feeble state it was evident that she would die if she were tormented. What her enemies wanted was a public death, a striking ceremonial which would appeal to the imagination of the crowd.

Her judges neglected nothing to cause her suffering. By a refinement of cruelty they took pleasure in describing to her the horrors of death by fire. This punishment was one of which she was particularly afraid.

"I would rather be decapitated,' she said, "than be burnt like that."

Far from being touched by her words, they insisted more and more. Weighed down by the weight of her chains, hemmed in on all sides by brutal enemies, at the bottom of an abyss of misery into which never a ray of pity or of hope descended, a cry of revolt sometimes came to her lips. She cried out to God, the great Judge, against the wrongs which were inflicted upon her, saying: "Those who desire my life may well find that they are endangering their own."

On another occasion she answered her questioner: "If you do that which you threaten against me it will be an evil day for your own body and soul."

As a matter of fact, many of her judges had a wretched end. All had to undergo public contempt and the reproaches of their own conscience. Cauchon died overwhelmed with remorse. The people dug up his body in order to throw it into a sewer. The promoter of the trial, Jean d'Estivet, died in the gutter. Several others appeared at the Process of Rehabilitation, twenty-five years later, rather in the character of the accused than as witnesses. Their attitude was piteous, while their language showed the trouble of their souls and the deep sense of their abasement.

Her enemies by no means respected truth in transcribing the words of the accused. One day when she was being interrogated on the subject of her visions, the replies which she had formerly given were read. Jean Lefevre observed and error of transcription and remarked it to Jeanne, who begged the scrivener, Menchon, to read it again. He read it over, and Jeanne declared that what she had said was exactly the contrary. Another time she said to them in a voice of reproach: "You write down all that there is against me, and nothing in my favour."

But, in spite of all, the superhuman energy of Jeanne, her inspired language, her greatness in her sufferings, ended in making an impression upon her judges. Cauchon felt deeply that she was an exceptional being, one who was inspired by Heaven. The hideous consequences of his crime began already to appear before him. At certain hours the voices of conscience murmured and threatened within him. Fear seized the prelate, but how could he escape? The English were there; they followed with feverish attention the course of the trial. They were waiting with sombre fury for the hour when they might immolate Jeanne after having tortured her and brought dishonour upon her. The Bishop of Beauvais could only see one way. It was to get the victim out of the way by assassination. Thus he might avoid a public crime by a secret one. He thought of poisoning her and actually sent her poison, which she ate. Immediately after taking it she was seized with extreme vomiting and fell ill. Her weakness was extreme. They feared for her life. She was surrounded by treacherous attentions because it would never do to allow her to die in so obscure a way. The English had paid dearly for her and they had marked her down for the scaffold. But her robust constitution triumphed and immediately the moral sufferings recommenced. They took advantage of her state of weakness. They redoubled their pressure. They demanded from her an abjuration. Nothing was spared to attain this end—spying, lying, attempts upon her honour, and even poison. The Maid whom a whole people adored was thus overwhelmed with ignominies by her judges and her jailers.

One scene—one might almost call it a comedy—was staged in the cemetery of Saint Ouen. There, within full view of the people and of the English soldiers, in the presence of her assembled judges at the head of whom were the Cardinal and four Bishops, Jeanne was requested to declare that she submitted herself to the Church. They pressed her, they implored her to have mercy upon herself, and not to force them to condemn her to the punishment of the fire. The executioner was, as a matter of fact, in his sinister cart at the very foot of the scaffold on which she was standing, and ready to conduct her, if she refused, to the old market-place where the stake awaited her.

And there, on that cloudy day, with the rain sweeping down like tears from heaven, under the weight of sadness which crept up from the tombs around, she was the victim of an immense sadness of soul. Her thoughts wandered away from this field of the dead. She saw once again the old land of Lorraine, the scattered groves where the birds sang and all the spots which she had loved in her youth. She thought she heard once more the songs of the farm-girls and of the shepherds. The sweet and plaintive notes seemed to be borne to her ears by the wind. She saw once more her thatched cottage, her mother and her old white-haired father whom she had seen last at Reims, and who would be so broken-hearted on learning of her death. There sprang up in her soul a great longing for life. To die at the age of twenty, was it not indeed cruel?

And for the first time the angel weakened. Christ also had His hour of weakness. On the Mount of

Olives had He not wished to push His terrible fate from Him? Did He not say, "If it be possible let this cup pass from me."

Jeanne, at the end of her strength, signed the document which they presented to her. Remember that she did not know how to read or to write. And remember, also, that the document which they forced her to sign was not that which they put upon the register. A wicked substitution took place. They did not even hesitate at this odious action. To-day it is clearly proved that the formula of abjuration which figured at the trial and is signed by a cross is a forgery. This formula is not, either in its contents or in its phrasing, that which Jeanne signed. Not one of the witnesses in the Process of Rehabilitation swore to the identity of this document, and five entirely denied it. The document which we possess now is extremely long. The three witnesses Delachambre, Taquel and Monnet have told us:

"We were all close by. We saw the document, and it was only five or six lines long." "The reading of it lasted about as long as a Paternoster," added Migiet.

Another witness declared:

"I know for a fact that the document which I read to Jeanne and which she signed is not that which is mentioned in the trial."

This last witness is none other than Massieu, the scrivener, who had caused Jeanne to pronounce the formula of Abjuration.

Jeanne in her distress neither heard nor understood this formula. She signed it without taking any oath and without having a full consciousness of what she was doing. She asserted this to her judges some days after, saying: "I never even heard what there was in this document of Abjuration. I have never meant to revoke anything which touches upon my relations with God."

Thus, that which threats, violence and torture could not obtain from her they got by their pleadings and by their hypocritical solicitations. This tender soul allowed herself to be influenced by a false semblance of sympathy and false signs of benevolence. But on that very night the Voices spoke once more imperiously in her prison, and on the 28th of May, Jeanne declared to her judges:

"My Voice has told me that it is treason to abjure. It is the truth that God sent me. That which I have done has been well done." And she put on once more the male attire which they had for a little time caused her to relinquish.

What happened after the Abjuration when, in spite of their promises to put her into and ecclesiastical prison and to have her guarded by a woman, they led her back into her vile dungeon? The following evidence in the Process of Rehabilitation will tell us.

"Jeanne told me that after her abjuration they had maltreated her in prison and beaten her, and that an English lord had insulted her. She said this publicly, and she told me that it was on account of this that she had again put on male attire."

And again:

"In my presence they asked Jeanne why she had once again dressed like a man. She replied that she had done it in self- defence, because she had no feeling of safety when dressed as a woman among the brutal guardians who surrounded her. Many others as well as myself were present at the time when she gave her reason for having put on this dress, affirming publicly that the English had been vile to her in the prison when she wore the dress of a woman. As a fact, I saw her in a sad state, her face stained with tears and so disfigured that I had deep pity for her."

Such is the deposition of Brother Sambard de la Pierre.

In this prison of the English, Jeanne drank the cup of bitterness to the last drop. She had sunk to the last gulf of human misery. All her sufferings were summed up in these words to her judges:

"I would rather die than stay longer in that prison."

And during these terrible hours, down in the castles of the Loire, Charles VII gave himself up to the pleasure of the dance and to all the joys of voluptuousness amid the languid sound of violas and of rebecks. In the midst of his feasts he had never a thought for her who had given him his crown.

In the presence of such facts one's thoughts grow sad and one's heart heavy. One might almost doubt eternal justice. Like the cry of agony from Jeanne, our own sad plaint rises up to the immense heavens and nothing but silence comes back to our appeal.

We can only look into ourselves and try to fathom the great mystery of grief. Is it not necessary for the beauty of souls and for the harmony of the universe? How could there be good without evil which serves as a contrast and shows us all the glory of it? Could one appreciate the benefit of light if one knew nothing of the night? Yes, the earth is the Calvary of the just, but it is also the school for heroism, virtue and genius. It is the vestibule of those glorious worlds where all pain which has been endured and all sacrifice which has been made prepare us for compensating joys. Souls are purified and embellished by grief. In the end those who are persecuted have the better of it. All pure hearts suffer in this world. Love is ever close to tears. At the bottom of human luxury there is nothing but emptiness and bitterness, and spectres glide amid our most voluptuous dreams.

All is a passing pageant in this world. Evil has only a short reign, and later, in the high spheres, the reign of pure justice spreads out into Eternity. No, the confidence of the faithful, the devotion of heroes and the hopes of martyrs are not vain things. The earth is but a stepping-stone to help us on the way to Heaven. May these sublime souls serve us as examples, and may their faith shine on us across the centuries. Let us chase from our hearts all sadness and vain discouragement. Let us know how to draw from our trials and difficulties all the fruit which they offer for our own improvement. Let us make ourselves worthy to be born again in those better worlds where there is no longer either hatred or injustice, or bitterness of heart, and where life is spent in a harmony which ever grows closer and a glory which ever increases.

∼

After her recantation Jeanne was declared to be a heretic, and a schismatic, and was therefore condemned without appeal. There was no hope now. She had to die, and die by fire. Such was the sentence of her judges. These judges, these orthodox men of the fifteenth century, would not recognize the mission of Jeanne d'Arc.

They were quite ready to believe in far-off manifestations of which the Bible speaks. They loved to talk of those distant epochs where messengers from on high had descended upon the earth and had mixed with mankind. They were willing, too, to believe in God Whom they placed far away in the depths of the heavens and to Whom they sent their empty prayers from day to day.

But for a God who lives and acts and shows Himself in this world in all the spontaneity, the youth and the freshness of life, and for great spirits who inspire their messengers with a breath of their own powerful being, they have nothing but hatred, insult and outrage.

The judges of Rouen and the Doctors of the University of Paris had declared Jeanne to be inspired by the devil.

And why? Because these representatives of the Orthodox formula and routine had only a surface knowledge, a knowledge which dries up the heart, deprives the thought of all nourishment, and in some cases leads to injustice and even to crime.

It is thus that at all epochs of the world's history, the narrow supporters of the law have been the destroyers of the ideal and of the divine. It is thus that under the iron will of despotism they have broken that which is the finest, the greatest and the most generous thing on earth. The results have been clear enough. They have been terrible for the Church. Here is what Henri Martin says on this matter:

"In condemning Jeanne the whole system of the Middle Ages, the doctrine of Innocent III and of the Inquisition, has pronounced its own condemnation. It had at first burned heretics, then it burned reformers who strove for a pure and moral Christianity, and finally, it had burned a prophet, a Messiah.

The spirit had gone out of it. From this time on, it was clearly a thing which worked against the progress of humanity and the manifestations of the government of Providence upon this earth."

Yes, humanity has gone forward. Progress has been realized in the world. No longer can the messengers of God be slain on the cross or amid the faggots. The dungeons and torture chambers have been shut; the gibbets have disappeared. But other weapons now have been turned against the inspired, who champion a new idea. Sarcasm, doubt, calumny, these are the formidable and eternal weapons which are used.

But if the terrible institutions of the Middle Ages, with all their list of punishments, the scaffolds and the stakes, have not been able to stop the march of truth, how can they hope to do it to-day?

The time has come when man in the region of thought asks for no other authority than his own conscience and his own intelligence. It is for this reason that we must insist upon our eternal right of judging and of understanding for ourselves.

The hour approaches, it is even now come, when all the errors of the past are leading up to a great day of reckoning before the Tribunal of history. Already the words and the actions of the great messengers, of the martyrs, and of the prophets are recalled and understood. Soon there will be a re-judgment of all our institutions. They will each be tested, and they will only preserve their moral power and their authority in so far as they have known how to give man greater latitude and power in his thoughts, and greater liberty to love, to rise and to progress.

11

ROUEN — THE PUNISHMENT

WE are now at the 30th of May, 1431. The drama draws to its end. It is eight o'clock in the morning. All the bells of the great Norman city send out a sad peal. It is the funeral chime—the chime of the dead. They tell Jeanne that her last hour has come.

"Alas!" she cried, weeping. "Do they really mean to treat me so cruelly that my virginal and uncorrupted body shall this very day be burned and reduced to ashes? Ah, rather would I be beheaded seven times than thus be burned... Oh, I call God to witness the great wrongs and injustice which they heap upon me!"

This thought of death by fire filled her with horror. She pictured in advance how the flames would mount around her, how slowly death would come upon her, how prolonged would be her agony, feeling ever these teeth of fire eating into her body. This death was that which was reserved for the worst criminals, and yet Jeanne, the innocent maid, Jeanne the liberator of a nation, was to undergo it.

Here was to be seen all the baseness of her enemies

—those enemies who she had so often beaten. Instead of according to her courage and her talents that homage which civilized soldiers give to their enemy when evil fortune delivers them into their hands, the English condemned Jeanne to an ignominious end after every possible ill-treatment. Her body should be consumed and her ashes cast into the Seine. There should be no tomb where those who loved her could weep, or which might remain as a center of memory for her admirers.

She mounted on her terrible chariot, and they led her to the place of punishment. Eight hundred English soldiers escorted her. A weeping crowd pressed round her as she passed. The procession came out through the Rue d'Écuyère on to the old market-place. There three stands had been erected. The prelates and the officers took their places on the two side galleries. Here on his throne, clad in his rope of purple, was the Cardinal of Winchester, with the Bishops of Beauvais and of Boulogne, all the judges, and the English leaders. Between these galleries the stake had been piled.

It was a huge heap of brushwood, so large that it dominated the whole picture. They designed that the punishment should be long, and that the Maid, overcome by her torture, should cry for mercy and should deny her mission and her Voices.

They read the act of accusation, an Act in seventy articles, in which was contained all that the most venomous hatred could invent to twist the facts in order to deceive public opinion, and to raise a feeling of horror against the victim. Jeanne knelt down. In this solemn moment in the presence of death her soul cleared itself from the earthly shadows. It saw before it the splendours of eternity. She prayed in a loud voice. Her prayer was long and fervent. She pardoned all her enemies and her executioners. In the sublime sweep of her thought and of her heart she reunited two nations, and drew together with her love two kingdoms. As she spoke emotion seized the crowd. Ten thousand people were sobbing round her. The judges themselves, those human tigers, Cauchon and Winchester, were moved to tears, but their emotion was a fleeting one. The Cardinal made a sign. Jeanne was tied to the fatal post by iron chains. Over her neck was passed a heavy collar.

At this moment she addressed Isambard de la Pierre, and said to him:

"I beg you, go and get the cross from that church there, and hold it up in front of my eyes until the moment of my death."

When they brought her the cross she wept and covered it with kisses. At the moment when she was to die this horrible death, deserted by all, she wished to have before her the image of that other Who had been punished yonder on the distant hill of the East, and Who had given His life also as a tribute to truth.

At this solemn hour she relived once more her short but brilliant life. She recalled the remembrance of all those whom she had loved, the peaceful days of her infancy at Domrémy, the sweet profile of her mother, the grave features of her father, the companions of her youth, Hauviette and Mengette, her uncle Durand Lexart, who accompanied her to Vaucouleurs, and the devouted men who had formed her escort on the road to Chinon.

In a rapid vision, the campaign of the Loire came clear before her, the glorious battles of Orleans, of Jargeau and of Patay, the brazen calls of the bugles and the joyous cries of the frenzied crowd.

All this she saw and heard once more in her last moments. As in a final embrace she wished to bid adieu to all these things and to all these people whom she had loved. Having none of them before her physical eyes, it was in the image of the dying Christ that she concentrated all these souvenirs, all these tender remembrances. It was to Him that she addressed her farewell to life amid the last throbs of her broken heart.

The executioners set light to the faggots and columns of smoke curled into the air. The flame rose and flickered through the piles of brushwood. The Bishop of Beauveais approached the foot of the scaffold and cried to her, "Abjure!" But Jeanne, already encircled with flame, replied:

"Bishop, I die at your hands, and I appeal from your judgment to that of God."

The flame, glowing and leaping, mounted and still mounted until it reached her pure body. Her garments smoked. She writhed in her iron bonds. Then her agonized voice cried out these final words to the silent and terrified crowd:

"Yes, my Voices came from on high. My Voices have not deceived me. My revelations were from God. All that which I have done I have done by the order of God." Her robe took fire and became one more flame amid the furnace. A last cry arose up—the supreme appeal of the martyr of Rouen to the Victim of Golgotha: "Jesus".

After that one heard nothing more save the crackling and roaring of the flame.

Jeanne is dead. The outer world is the brighter for her presence. She rises above the earthly vapours. She soars, leaving behind her a brilliant train. She is no longer a material being but a pure spirit, an ideal being of purity and of light. For her the heavens are open in their infinite depths. Legions of radiant spirits advance to meet her, and to escort her, and the hymn of triumph, the chant of celestial welcome, resounds.

"Greeting, greeting to the crowned martyr, greeting to you who by your sacrifice have won an eternal glory."

Jeanne has gone back into the bosom of God, into that inextinguishable centre of energy and intelligence and love which animates the whole universe with its vibrations. For a long time she remained there, then at last she came forth, more shining and more powerful, ready for missions of another sort of which we may speak further.

And God in reward has given her authority over her sisters of Heaven.

~

We may well pause here, and salute this noble virginal figure, this great-hearted girl, who after having saved France died before her twentieth year.

Her life shines like a ray from Heaven in the dreadful night of the Middle Ages.

She had come to bring to mankind, through her powerful faith and her confidence in God, the courage and the energy necessary to surmount a thousand obstacles. She had come to bring to France, in abasement and agony, hope and salvation. As a reward for her heroic unselfishness she had, alas! received only bitter humiliation and treachery, and the crown of her short but marvellous career was a passion and death so sad, that they have only been equalled by that of the Christ.

The father of Jeanne, struck to the heart by the news of the martyrdom of his child, died suddenly, and was followed almost immediately by the elder of his sons. The mother had thenceforth but one aim in this life, which was to persist in procuring the revision of the trial. She made attempt after attempt. She addressed request after request to the King and to the Pope, for a long time in vain.

In 1449, when Charles VII made his entry into Rouen, she had some hopes, but the Pope, Nicholas V, gave evasive replies, and the King remained confirmed in his ingratitude. In 1455, with Calixtus III, she was more successful, for the whole people of France supported her appeal. The Court was compelled to listen to the voice of the public. They had, at last, made the King understand that his honour was touched by the accusation of heresy which had served as a pretext for the heroine's death.

The rehabilitation was carried out rather in the interests of the Crown of France than out of respect for the memory of Jeanne. In these later days the Church has learnt how to exploit her ancient victim.

At all times, Jeanne has been sacrificed to the interest of cause and of party. But there are thousands of obscure and humble souls who have learned to love her for herself. Their thoughts of love mount towards her, across the gulf of space. She is far more conscious of those than of the pompous manifestations organized in her honour. They are her true joy and her sweet remembrance, as she has told me many time in the intimacy of our psychic reunion.

∼

Jeanne has long been misunderstood and unrecognized. She is so still by many of those who profess to admire her, but one must admit that the error is natural. It arises from the fact that those who had made her a victim, and the King among them, in order to conceal their crime from the eyes of posterity, did all they could to misrepresent the part she played, to minimize her mission and to hand a veil round her memory. It was for this reason that they destroyed the register of the proceedings of Poitiers, that certain documents of the trial at Rouen, according to Quicherat, were falsified, and that the witnesses of the Process of Rehabilitation were reported with a constant idea of making things easier for those in authority.

It was said in the records of Rouen that on the very morning of her punishment, in her last examination which was undergone in prison without any scrivener being present and quoted only by Cauchon some days later, Jeanne had denied her Voices. It is false. She never denied her Voices. In one moment of weakness she had submitted herself to the Church. In that act alone lies what they have called "The Abjuration of St. Ouen."

It is through misrepresentations of this sort that the shadow has so long darkened the memory of Jeanne. At the beginning of the nineteenth century there remained only a feeble remembrance of her, an incomplete and shadowy legend. But the justice of history has willed that the truth should come to the light of day. From the ranks of the people there have risen up persevering students—Michelet, Henri Martin, Senator Fabre, above all, Quicherat, Director of the School of Records. There were priests also among them. All these conscientious workers have carefully scrutinized the yellow parchments, thick with the dust of libraries. Many unknown manuscripts have been discovered. They have found in the Royal Ordinance of that time, in the Chronicles of St. Denis, and in a number of archives deposited at the Library of Records, and among the ministerial documents of the loyal towns, the revelation of facts which at last do justice to the heroine. This justice has come late, but it is brilliant, absolute and universally admitted.

And that is why modern France has a great duty—the duty of repairing, morally at any rate, the faults of ancient France. The thoughts of all should be turned towards this noble and pure image, towards this radiant figure which is that of the Angel of the Fatherland. All children of France should bear in their thoughts and in their hearts the remembrance of her whom Heaven sent to us at the hour of our disasters and of our destruction. Across the ages an eternal homage should mount towards this brave spirit who loved France, even to death, who pardoned on the scaffold all the desertions and all the treacheries which she had endured, and offered herself up as a holocaust for the safety of a people.

The sacrifice of Jeanne d'Arc had an immense effect. In politics, it brought about the unity of France. Before her time we were a country which was dislocated and torn by faction. After her time there existed a solid France. Jeanne had gone down to her death, but through her inspiring soul the national unity had been attained.

Every work of salvation is carried through by sacrifice, the greater the sacrifice the more supreme and imposing the work. Every mission of redemption is finished and crowned by a martyrdom. It is the great law of history. It was with Jeanne as it was with Christ. It is through this that one's life carries the divine seal. God, the sovereign Artist, reveals Himself by incontestable and sublime signs.

The sacrifice of Jeanne had another, even vaster meaning. It will remain a sign and example for generations and centuries to come. God has His object in putting such lessons before humanity. It is always to these great figures that the thoughts of all those who suffer, and of all those who bend under the burden of sorrow, must turn. They are so many furnaces of energy and of moral beauty, where souls frozen by the chill of adversity may warm themselves once more. Across the centuries they throw a luminous trail, a track which leads and guides us towards regions of glory. Such souls have come upon earth in order to make us realize the other world. Their death has been the nurse of life and their memory has comforted thousands of the sad and the needy.

12

JOAN'S SECRET POWER

THE phenomena of clairvoyance, clairaudience and prophecy which appear in the life of Jeanne d'Arc have given rise to most diverse explanations. Among historians, some have seen in them a case of hallucination. Some have gone so far as to speak of hysteria and neurosis. Others again have attributed a supernatural and miraculous character to these facts.

The essential object of this work is to analyse these phenomena, to show that they are real and that they are governed by laws which have long been ignored, but which are now being slowly unfolded in the most impressive and detailed fashion.

In proportion as our knowledge of the universe and of ourselves increases the idea of the supernatural recedes and vanishes. One realizes now that Nature is one, but that in its immensity it contains great kingdoms and forms of life which have long escaped our senses. These senses are most limited. They only allow us to perceive the most obvious things, the elementary constituents of the universe and of life. Their utter poverty was revealed when more powerful optical instruments—the telescope and the microscope—appeared, for these have enlarged in either direction the field of our visual perspective. What did we know of those innumerable existences which live around and even within us?

These things, however, are only the substratum of life, but above us sphere follows sphere. Each contains forms of life delicately graduated from subtle ethereal intelligences of a human or even subhuman character, up to the regions of the angels, but all belonging to imponderable states of matter which science has now defined in many aspects, as, for example, in the radioactivity of bodies, the Rontgen rays and in all those new developments which throw a light upon radiant matter.

Outside those visible and tangible forms with which we are familiar, we know now that matter is to be found in many varied states, invisible and imponderable, refining itself more and more, and turning itself into force and into light until it becomes the cosmic ether of the physicists. In all these varied states and under all these aspects, it is still the substance in which innumerable organisms have birth, and which produces forms of an unimaginable delicacy. Within this ocean of subtle matter there is an intense life about and around us. Outside the narrow circle of our normal senses there are great gulfs opening out, and a vast unknown world can dimly be seen, peopled by forces and beings which we cannot perceive, but which, none the less, take a share in our joys, as in our sufferings, and can even to a certain extent influence and help us. It is into this wonderful world that a new science is striving to penetrate.

At a meeting held at the Psychological Institute

some years ago, Dr. Duclaux, Director of the Pasteur Institute, expressed himself in these words:

"This world, peopled by influences which we encounter without knowing it, penetrated by that Divine impulse which we feel without being able to define, is more interesting than the sphere to which our minds have hitherto been confined. Let us try to open it up by our researches. Immense discoveries are to be made there by which humanity will profit."

Marvel of marvels! We ourselves belong in the most important part of our being to this invisible world which is slowly revealing itself to attentive observers. There is in each human being a fluid form, a subtle body, indestructible, an exact image of the physical body which is only its outer clothing. This form has its own senses, more delicate than those of the physical body which are indeed only a feeble reflexion of the psychic.

The existence of this double or phantom of a living presence is established by innumerable facts and witnesses. It can disengage itself from its fleshly envelope during sleep, whether it be natural sleep or hypnotic, and so show itself at a distance. The cases of telepathy, the phenomena of duplication and of materialization, the apparition of living people at points far from the spot where their bodies are lying, chronicled so many times by F. Myers, C. Flammarion, Professor Charles Richet, Dr. Darriex, Dr. Maxwell, and others, have established the fact beyond all question. The records of the Society of Psychic Research of London, collected by eminent English authorities, are rich in facts of this description.

The fluidic body is the true seat of our faculties and of our consciousness, and is that which the religious in all ages have called the soul. The soul is not a vague metaphysical entity, but rather a personal centre of force, and of life which is for ever contained within its subtle form. It pre-existed before our birth, and death has no effect upon it. It finds itself on the other side of the tomb with all its intellectual and moral acquisitions still intact. Its destiny is to pursue across time and space its evolution towards ever higher states, always growing brighter in the light of justice, truth and personal beauty. The entity reaps in its psychic state the fruits of all the labours, the sacrifices, and the griefs of its successive existences.

Those who have lived with us and who then continue their evolution in space do not lose their sympathy for our sufferings and our tears. From the higher planes of the universal life there sweep down for ever upon earth currents of strength and inspiration. Thence come the sudden illuminations of genius, the overpowering inspirations which sway a nation in some hour of doom. Thence, also, come help and comfort for those who bend under the burden of existence. A mysterious tie unites the visible and the invisible. Relations can be established between the spheres of life by the help of certain specially endowed people who are able to waken and bring into action those psychic senses and those deeper vibrations which exist in every human being. These helpers are those whom we call sensitives or mediums.

∼

In the days of Jeanne d'Arc these things were not known. People had only confused ideas as to the universe and the true nature of our being. On many points these ideas were incomplete or erroneous, but since then, from century to century, the human spirit, in spite of hesitations and uncertainties, has risen from one conquest to another. Now it begins to soar. Human thought rises. We begin to look above the physical world and to plunge into the vast depths of the psychic, where one may trace the cause of causes, the key of all mysteries, the solution of the great problems of life, of death and of destiny.

One is aware of the opposition which these studies have encountered. Critics even now attack those who courageously persevere in their researches into our relation with the Invisible. But has there not been a similar contempt, even among learned societies, for many discoveries which have been universally accepted later as brilliant truths? It will be the same in this case of the existence of spirits. One after another, men of science have been obliged to admit it, frequently as the result of experiments which were devised in order to demonstrate the opposite. Sir William Crookes, the celebrated English chemist, some of whose compatriots think him the equal of Newton, is one of these. So also are Russel Wallace and Oliver Lodge, Lombroso in Italy, Dr. Paul Gibier and Darriex in France, State Councillor Aksakof in Russia, in Germany Baron du Prel and the Physicist Zollner.

The sober man who holds a position mid-way between credulity and equally blind incredulity is compelled to recognize that these phenomena have appeared at every epoch. You will find them in all ages of history, and in the sacred books of all people. The psychics of India, Egypt, Greece and Rome share the experiences of the mediums of our own day. The Prophets of Judea, the Christian Apostles, the Druidesses of Gaul, the inspired peasants in the Cevennes at the time of the War of the Camisards, all drew their revelations from the same source as our Maid of Lorraine.

Psychic power has always existed, for man has always been a spirit, and this spirit holds open at every epoch of the world's history a channel which leads to regions untouched by our ordinary senses.

Constant and permanent, these phenomena reproduce themselves in every country and under every form, sometimes, it must be admitted, common and crude, like the tilting of tables, the movement of objects without contact and the haunting of houses, but also in more delicate and sublime phases such as ecstasy, or high inspiration. These differences depend upon the quality of the intelligences which are acting upon the medium.

The experiences of that illustrious man of science, Sr. W. Crookes, are upon record. For three years he obtained in his own house the materializations of the spirit Katie King under conditions of strict control. Crookes, speaking of these manifestations, said, "I do not say that it is possible. I say that it actually is so."

Some have pretended that Crookes retracted. It was not so. Mr. Stead wrote to the New York American: "London. Feb. 9, 1909. I have seen Sir W. Crookes, and he authorizes me to say, 'Since my original experiences in Spiritualism thirty years ago I have never had occasion to modify the opinions which I formed.'"

Oliver Lodge, formerly Rector of the University of Birmingham and Fellow of the Royal Society wrote: "I have been led to absolute certainty upon the question of survival by proofs which rest upon purely scientific basis."

Frederic Myers, of Cambridge, who was elected as Honorary President by the Official International Congress of Psychology of Paris in 1900, lays it down in his great book, "Human Personality", that the voices and messages come from the Beyond. Speaking of Mrs. Thompson the medium he says, "I believe that the greater part of these messages come from Spirits which make temporary use of the organism of mediums in order to send them."

The famous Professor Lombroso of Turin declared in "La Lettura": "The cases of haunted houses in which for years apparitions and noises made themselves manifest as a sequence to tragic deaths—facts which are independent of the presence of mediums—argue in favour of the intervention of the dead. There are many cases where such phenomena have been known to extend over several generations and even over several centuries." (See Annales des Sciences psychiques. Feb. 1908).

One cannot but realize the importance of such witnesses. We could quote many more if the scope of this book would permit it.

We will now turn to the phenomena which occurred in the life of Jeanne d'Arc, and we will examine them. They are of vital importance, for it was by her extraordinary psychic faculties that she was enabled to acquire her rapid ascendancy over the army and the people. They looked upon her as a being endowed with supernatural powers. The army was a mere collection of adventurers and brigands drawn together by the lure of plunder. Every sort of vice abounded amid these undisciplined troops, who were always ready to disband. It was amidst these shameless rapscallions that this young girl, eighteen years of age, had to live. Out of such ruffians, who had no respect even for the name of God, she had to make whole-hearted idealists, ready to sacrifice all for a noble and holy cause.

This miracle she was able to accomplish. It was thought at first that she was one of those women who are to be found among the camp followers of armies. But soon her inspired words, her austere manners, her sobriety, and the wonders which occurred in her presence, impressed these rude minds. The army and the people were led to look upon her as a sort of fairy or good genius. They spoke of her as one of those fantastic creatures who haunt the springs and the woods.

Her task, however, became ever harder. She had to make herself respected and loved as a leader and, at the same time, she had to induce these grim fighting men to recognize in her the image of France—of the fatherland which she longed to restore.

By the realization of her prophecies and by her wonderful deeds she gradually inspired them with absolute confidence. They came to look on her as something almost divine. Her presence was to them a guarantee of victory and a symbol of celestial help. Loving her and trusting her, they were more loyal to her than the King or the nobles. On seeing her, their gross thoughts and their evil passions were hushed, and gave place to veneration. All looked upon her as a superhuman being. This is shown by the evidence of Jean Aulon at the trial. Count Guy de Laval, after seeing her at Selles-sur-Cher, when with the Court of the King, wrote to his mother (June 8, 1429), "It is a truly divine thing to see and to hear her."

Without occult help how could a simple country girl acquire such prestige and attain such success? All she had known of war during her youth – the perpetual alarms of the peasants, the sacked villages, the groans of the wounded and dying, the roaring of the flames—would rather tend to repel her from the career of arms. But she was chosen from on high to raise

France from her abasement and to instill the idea of Country into every heart. It was for this that these marvelous gifts and this immense support were granted.

Let us examine more closely the nature and the range of the psychic faculties of Jeanne. First of all, there were these mysterious voices which she used to hear in the silence of the woods, in the midst of the tumult of battle, in the depths of her dungeon, and even in the presence of her judges. These voices were often accompanied by visions, as she herself stated in the course of a dozen different cross-examinations. Then there were the cases of prophecy, correctly announcing facts of the future.

Are these facts authentic? On this point there cannot be the slightest doubt. The testimony and the documents still exist. The letters and the chronicles abound with the evidence.

Above all, there is the Trial at Rouen, the records of which, though compiled by the enemies of the accused girl, testify even more strongly in her favour than those which came to light in the Process of Rehabilitation. In the latter the same facts are attested under oath by witnesses giving evidence before a solemn tribunal.

Above all these I would place the opinion of one who sums them all up, and whose authority is unique. I speak of Quicherat, Director of the School of Archives. He was not a mystic or an occult student; he was a grave, cold man and an eminent historical critic. He devoted himself to a profound research and a scrupulous examination of the life of Jeanne d'Arc. This is what he says:

"Whether science can account for it or not, one is compelled none the less to accept the truth of her visions."

To this I would add that the new sciences can account for it. For all these phenomena, which in those days were considered so miraculous, can be clearly explained to-day by the laws of mediumship.

Jeanne was ignorant. Her only books had been Nature and the starry sky. To Pierre de Versailles, who asked her at Poitiers as to the state of her education, she replied: "I do not know either A or B." Many gave evidence as to this during the Process of Rehabilitation.

In spite of her ignorance, she had undertaken the most marvelous work that a woman had ever accomplished. In carrying it through she was fated to show rare knowledge and skill. An unlettered girl, she was destined to confound and conquer the doctors of Poitiers. By her military genius and the cleverness of her plans she acquired complete influence over the chiefs and the soldiers. At Rouen she contended against sixty learned men, skilful theologians, she avoided all their traps and replied to all their objections. More than once she embarrassed them by her retorts, rapid as lightning and piercing as a sword-point.

Now, how can one reconcile so marked a superiority of character with her want of education? Surely it is that there is another source of knowledge besides school learning. It was by constant communication with the invisible world from the age of thirteen, when her first vision occurred, that Jeanne acquired the powers which were indispensable for the accomplishment of her arduous task. The lessons of our unseen guides are more effective than those of a professor, and more fruitful in moral revelations. Those highways of knowledge, the universities and the Churches, are not opened up by such means. Their representative men read but seldom in that "Book of God" of which

Jeanne speaks, that great book of the invisible universe whence she had gained wisdom and light:

"There is more in the book of Our Lord than in your books. I have a book which no clerk has ever read, however great a clerk he may be," said she at Poitiers.

By this she means that the occult and divine worlds possess sources of truth richer and more profound than those from which human beings can draw, and that those sources are often open to the simple, the humble, the ignorant, and those whom God has marked with His seal. They find there elements of knowledge surpassing all those which study can gain for us.

Human knowledge is allied to pride; its development is associated almost always with pedantry and convention. It often lacks clearness and simplicity. Certain works of psychology, for example, are so obscure, so complicated, and bristling with so many difficult words that they become ridiculous. It is amusing to notice what efforts of the imagination and what intellectual gymnastics men like Professor Flournoy and Dr. Grasset have to use in order to bolster up theories which are as absurd as they are abstruse. Those truths, however, which come from high revelation appear in brilliant clearness. In a few words uttered by mouths of simple people they cut through the most difficult problems. "I thank thee, Father," said Christ, "Thou has hid these things from the wise and prudent, and hast revealed them unto babes."

Bernardin de Saint Pierre expresses the same thought: "To find the truth one must search for it with a simple heart."

It was, then, with a simple heart that Jeanne listened to her Voices, that she asked them questions in important cases, and confided in their wise direction until under the impulse of higher forces she became an admirable instrument endowed with precious psychic faculties. Not only was she clairvoyant and clairaudient, but her touch and her sense of smell were affected by the visions which appeared before her.

"I have touched Saint Catherine when she stood in front of me," said she.

"Have you kissed or embraced Saint Catherine or Saint Margaret?" they asked her.

"I have embraced them both."

"Were they fragrant?"

"It is good to know that they were indeed fragrant."

In another examination she expressed herself thus:

"I saw Saint Margaret and the angels with the eyes of my body as clearly as I see you, and when they left me I wept, and I dearly wished that they could have taken me with them."

This is a reaction which is felt by every medium who comes in contact with the splendours of the Beyond, and the radiant beings who live there. They experience a sense of ecstasy which makes the realities of life sadder and more heavy. To participate for one instant in the celestial life and then to fall heavily back into the shadows of our world, what a bitter contrast!

This was especially so in the case of Jeanne, whose exquisite soul, after finding itself for a moment in surroundings which corresponded with itself, and having received "great comfort," saw itself once more faced by the hard and rough duties which had been laid upon her.

Few men understand these things. The vulgarities of the earth conceal the beauties of this invisible world which surrounds us, and in which we live as blind folk might in the midst of Light. But there are delicate souls, beings endowed with subtle senses, for who this thick veil of material things occasionally opens.

Through these openings they catch a glimpse of the corner of the divine outer world, the world of true joy and of lasting happiness in which we shall all find ourselves after death, free and happy in proportion as we have lived, loved and suffered.

It was not only through these extraordinary facts, the visions and voices, that Jeanne learned to place implicit confidence in her invisible friends. Her reason also showed her that the source of her inspirations was pure and elevated, for her Voices guided her always towards useful action associated with devotion and self-sacrifice. While certain mystics lose themselves in barren meditations, in the case of Jeanne psychic phenomena all tended towards the realization of a great task. Hence came her invincible faith.

"I believe as firmly," said she to her judges, "in the doings and the sayings of St. Michael, who has appeared to me, as I believe that our Lord Jesus Christ has suffered death and the passion for us, and that which compels me to believe it is the good advice, the comfort and the proofs which he has given me."

In her judgment it was the moral side of these manifestations which constituted a proof and guarantee of their authenticity. By their good advice, by their constant support, and by the wise instructions which they gave her, she recognized in her guides missioners from on high.

In the course of her trial as well as in her warlike operations these Voices advised her what to do or say. She had recourse to them in all cases of difficulty.

"I asked advice from the Voice as to what I ought to answer, asking It in turn to take counsel with our Lord, and the Voice answered me, 'Speak out bravely, God will aid you,'"

Her judges interrogated her on this point.

"How do you explain that your Saints can answer you?"

"When I make a request to Saint Catherine," Jeanne replied, "then she and Saint Margaret make the same request to God, and then, by permission of God, they give me the reply."

Thus for all those who know how to ask help from the invisible with humility and prayer, the Divine Thought streams through sphere to sphere from the height of space down to the depth of humanity. But all cannot see this as Jeanne did.

When the Voices were silent she refused to reply upon any important question.

"I cannot answer you that yet. I have not had God's permission."

"I feel that I cannot fully tell you all that I know. I have a very great fear of doing wrong by saying something which may be displeasing to my Voices, who may not wish that I should give you an answer."

Admirable discretion which many would do well to imitate when the voices of wisdom and of conscience do not order them to speak!

To the very end of her tragic life Jeanne showed a great love for her invisible guides and complete confidence in their protection. Even when they seemed to abandon her after having promised her safety she did not make any complaint or utter any reproach.

By her own account they had said to her in her prison: "You will be delivered by a great victory," and instead of deliverance it was death which came. Her inquisitors, who neglected no means of making her despair, insisted on this apparent abandonment.

Jeanne replied cheerfully and without reproach that she would submit herself to the will of God.

13

WHAT WERE HER VOICES?

THE record of the Saint of Lorraine presented so many cases of clairvoyance and of prophecy that they gave her by common consent the right to claim that she had the mysterious power of divination. Sometimes she seemed to read the future, as for example when she said to the soldier at Chinon who cursed her at the moment of her entrance into the castle:

"Ah, you make light of God, and yet you are so near your death."

That same evening this soldier was drowned by accident. So was it also in the case of the Englishman, Glasdale, at the attack on the tower of the bridge before Orleans. She summoned him to appear before the King of Heaven, adding "I have great pity for your soul." At the same instant, Glasdale fell with all his armour into the Loire, where he was drowned.

Later, at Jargeau, she saw the danger of the Duke d'Alencon, over whose safety she had promised to watch.

"Gentle Duke," she cried, "retire from where you stand, for if not that cannon down yonder will be the death of you."

This foresight proved to be correct, for the Lord of Lude who took the place abandoned by the Duke was killed immediately afterwards.

At other times, and frequently, she was warned by her Voices.

At Vaucouleurs, without ever having seen him, she went straight up to the Lord of Baudricourt:

"I recognized him," she explained, "because my Voice told me. It said to me, 'There he is.'"

After this opening Jeanne predicted to him the deliverance of Orleans, the consecration of the King at Reims, and finally told him of the defeat of the French on the Day of Harengs at the very moment when it was taking place. At Chinon, when brought into the presence of the King, Jeanne had no difficulty in picking him out from the three hundred courtiers amidst whom he was concealed.

"When I entered into the chamber of the King," said she, "I recognized him among the others on account of my Voices, which revealed him to me."

In a private conversation she told him the very words of a prayer which he had addressed to God when he was alone in his Oratory. Her Voices told her that the sword of Charles Martel was buried in the Church of Saint Catherine de Fierbois, and caused her to send and get it.

Again it was her Voices which awoke her at Orleans when, overcome with fatigue, she had thrown herself upon a bed and knew nothing of the attack upon the castle of Saint Loup.

"My Voices tell me that I must go against the English," she suddenly cried. "You did not tell me that the blood of France is being poured."

Jeanne knew, because she had been warned by her guides, that she would be wounded by an arrow at the attack of Tourelles, 7th May, 1429. A letter from the representative of Brabant, which is preserved in the archives of Brussels (dated 22nd April that same year, so that it was written fifteen days before the event), related this prophecy and the manner in which it would be fulfilled. On the eve of the battle Jeanne said again:

"To-morrow my blood will be shed."

On this same day she predicted against all probability that the triumphant army would enter into Orleans over the bridge which at that time was broken down. That is what did occur.

When the town was delivered Jeanne insisted that the King should not delay his departure for Reims, repeating, "I will only be with you for one year. It is needful, then that you use me to the full."

What foresight as to her own short career!

She was also warned by her Voices of the coming surrender of Troyes, and later of her own captivity.

"In Easter week when I was near the moat of Melun my Voices told me that I should be taken before the feast of S. John," said she to her judges at Rouen, "and I prayed then that when taken I should die at once rather than linger in the torments of a prison. They answered me, "Take everything as it comes. It is needful that it should be as we say'. But they did not tell me the exact hour." In this connection we may quote her striking reply to her inquisitors, "If I had known the hour I would not have gone if only my own free will were concerned. None the less, I would have done what was ordered by my Voices, come what might."

They tell also of a touching scene in the church of Compiègne. She said, weeping, to those around her:

"Dear friends and comrades, they will sell and betray me. Soon I shall be handed over for execution. Pray for me."

In prison her guides told her to her great joy of the relief of Compiègne. She had also a revelation of her own tragic end in a form which she did not understand, but which her judges read clearly.

"My Voices told me also that I should be delivered. They added, 'Take all in good part, do not trouble over your sufferings. Through them you will come at last to the Kingdom of Paradise'."

Often these Voices told her of the secret councils which were held by the jealous captains, which they concealed from her in order that they might discuss privately the state of the war. But suddenly Jeanne would appear. She had learned in advance what their plots had been and she would frustrate them.

"You have been at your council, and I have been at mine. The council of God will be fulfilled. Yours will come to nought."

Was it not also to the inspiration of her guides that Jeanne owed those eminent qualities which make the great general knowledge of strategy and cleverness in using artillery—a thing which at that age was new?

How was it that she knew that the French preferred to fight in the open rather than to defend ramparts? And how could it be explained in any normal way that a simple young shepherdess should become in a single day an incomparable leader and a consummate general?

Her mediumship took varied forms. These faculties, which are scattered and attenuated among many individuals in our time, were all united in her, forming a single powerful whole.

They were also increased by her great moral strength. The heroine was the interpreter and the agent of a world which is invisible, subtle, etheric, extending over and above our own and communicating its vibrations, its harmonies and its Voices to certain human beings specially endowed to receive them.

The phenomena which filled the life of Jeanne all made for a single end. The mission imposed upon her by those high beings, whose nature and character it is beyond us to define, was definite and precise. It was announced beforehand and was carried out upon those very lines. All her history bore witness to it. To the judges at Rouen, she said:

"I have come from God, I have nothing to do here. Send me back to God from Whom I have come."

And when on the scaffold the flames roared around her, she cried still: "Yes, my Voices were from God. My Voices have not deceived me."

Could Jeanne be lying? Her sincerity, her sense of right, which showed themselves in every action of her life, give the answer. A soul so loyal as hers, which was ready to accept any sacrifice rather than deny France or her King, could not stoop to falsehood. There is such an accent of truth and conviction in her words that no one, even among her most bitter enemies, could accuse her of imposture.

Anatole France, who certainly does not mince his words, writes:

"That which stands out in the whole narrative is that she was a saint. She was a saint, with all the attributes of the sanctity of the fifteenth century. She had visions, and these visions were neither false nor counterfeit."

And later he says: "No one can suspect her of falsehood."

Her loyalty was complete. In order to support her Voices she did not make use, as so many people do, of excessive or extravagant terms. "She never swore," said one witness on the Process of Rehabilitation, and when she wished to give emphasis she was content to add "Without fail." These words are to be found also in the Interrogatory of the Rouen Trial. They have a particular meaning in her mouth when said in her frank voice and with that honest bearing which was so characteristic of her.

Then, again, was she deceived? Her good sense, her clearness of mind, her sure judgment, the flashes of genius which continually illumined her life, make it impossible to believe it. Jeanne was not the victim of hallucination. None the less, some critics have believed it. Most of the physiologists, for example, Pierre Janet, Ribot and Dr. Grasset, as well as the alienists, including Dr. Lelut, Calmeil and others, can only see in mediumship a form of hysteria or neurosis. In their eyes clairvoyants are pathological, and Jeanne d'Arc herself does not escape their censure. Quite recently, Professor Morselli, in his pamphlet "Psychology and Spiritualism", has taken the view that mediums are weak or unstable natures.

It is always easy to describe as mistakes, hallucinations or madness, those facts with which we are not in sympathy or which we cannot explain. Many skeptics think themselves clear-headed when they are in truth simply the dupes of their own prejudices.

Jeanne was neither hysterical nor neurotic. She was strong and enjoyed perfect health. Her manners were chaste, and although she was most attractive in appearance, her bearing imposed respect and veneration even upon the ruffians with whom she was brought into contact. She stood without weakening the greatest possible fatigue.

"She has just passed nearly six days under arms," wrote, on the 21st June, 1429, Percival de Bourganvilliers, Chamberlain of Charles VII, "and when she was on horseback she roused the admiration of her companions in arms by the length of time she could remain in the saddle without being forced to dismount."

Her endurance is proved by many witnesses.

"She carried herself in such a fashion," said the Chevalier Thibault d'Armagnac, "that no man could possibly bear the hardships of war better than she." All her captains marveled at the pains and fatigues which she endured.

The same may be said as to her austerity. We have many witnesses on this point, some of whom lived with her for a time like Dame Colette, and others who habitually surrounded her. Let us quote the words of her page, Louis de Contes: Jeanne was very self-denying. Often in a whole day she only ate a morsel of bread. I wondered that she should eat so little. When she was leading her ordinary life she never ate more than twice a day."

The marvelous rapidity with which our heroine was cured of her wounds shows also that she had a powerful vitality. Only a few days would suffice and she was back in the field of battle. After having sprung from the tower of Beau Revoir and being seriously injured she was back in her ordinary health as soon as she could take some nourishment.

Do facts like these show a feeble or a nervous nature?

And if from these physical qualities we pass to those of the spirit the same conclusion holds good. The numerous phenomena of which she had been the centre, far from troubling her reason, as is the case in hysterical people, seemed on the contrary to have strengthened it, if one may judge by the lucid, short, decisive and unexpected replies which she made to her questioners at Rouen. Her memory remained sure, her judgment sound. She had preserved the thoroughness of her intellectual faculties and the command of herself.

Dr. J. Dumas, Professor at the Sorbone, in a note published by Anatole France at the end of his second volume, declares that he has not found, in all the testimony concerning Jeanne, any of the recognized signs of hysteria. He insists at some length on the objective character of the phenomena, on the complete independence of the seeress from the saints whom she saw. It does not seem that these conditions could be in any way related to any recognized pathological type.

"There is nothing," says Andrew Lang, "which would lead us to think that Jeanne, while she was in communion with her saints, found herself out of her own body or unconscious of that which surrounded her. On the contrary we see that in the terrible scene of her abjuration she could hear at the same time with equal clearness the voices of her saints and the sermon of the preacher, the errors of which she was able to point out."

We may add that never at any time was she obsessed, since her spirits only came at certain moments and usually when she herself called them, whereas obsession is characterized by the constant and unavoidable presence of invisible beings.

The Voices of Jeanne have always some connection

with her great mission; what they say is never puerile. They have always a reason for coming. They do not contradict themselves, and they do not stultify themselves by the erroneous beliefs of those days, as would have been natural if Jeanne were predisposed to hallucination. Far from giving faith to the hobgoblins, to the virtues of the Mandragora, and to the hundred other false ideas of that epoch, she shows in her Interrogatory her ignorance on these points, or else indicates the contempt with which she regarded them.

In the case of Jeanne there was none of that egotistical feeling, none of that conceit which characterizes hallucinated people, who usually attribute great importance to their own little person and imagine that they are surrounded by enemies and persecutors. Under her divine inspiration her thoughts were turned only towards France and her King.

The great alienist, Pierre de Boismont, who made an effective study of the question, sees in Jeanne a high degree of independence of mind. None the less, he thinks there is an element of hallucination in the phenomena which surround her, but he gives them a physiological rather than a pathological explanation. By that he means that these hallucinations have not prevented her from retaining a perfectly sane mind. They were the outcome of mental exaltation, which had in it nothing morbid. According to him the conception of a directing idea had formed itself in the brain of Jeanne, and he sees in her a chosen soul, one of those "Messengers who are sent to us from the mysterious depths of the Infinite."

Without being of the same opinion as the celebrated Salpêtrière expert as to the determining causes of these phenomena, Dr. Dupouy attributes them to the influence of celestial beings, and comes to the same general conclusion. In his opinion, however, the imagination of Jeanne had the effect of making those angelic personalities, who served her as guides, objective. We may adopt this method of looking at the matter, since we know that she considered these saints as being the same as those whose images decorated the Church of Domrémy.

But again I ask: How could one attribute to hallucination Voices which awoke her in her sleep in order to warn her of present or future events, as was the case at Orleans and during her trial at Rouen? How, too, could we imagine this in the case of voices which advised her to act entirely differently from the way in which she would wish? During her captivity in the tower of Beau Revoir she received much advice from her guides, who desired to save her from making a mistake, but none the less they could not prevent her from springing from the top of the tower, and she lived to repent it.

To say with Lavisse, Anatole France and others, that the Voices heard by Jeanne was that of her own conscience seems to be equally at variance with the facts. Everything shows that the Voices were exterior to herself. The phenomena was not within her own mind, since she was awakened, as we have seen, by the appeals of her guides and sometimes could only catch the last few words of what they said.

She could only hear them well in hours of silence, as Anatole France remarks: "The turmoil of the prison and the noises of her guards" prevented her from understanding the words. There is, then, every evidence that they came from without. A noise would not stand in the way of an internal voice which was speaking in the secrecy of one's own soul.

Let us, then, end our examination by realizing once

for all that in Jeanne we are in the presence of a great medium.

With all respect to Dr. Morselli and so many others, mediumship does not show itself only in the case of feeble spirits or of minds which have a tendency to madness.

There are geniuses of many orders, Petrarch, Pascal, Lafontaine, Goethe, Sardou, Flammarion, and also men penetrated with a divine spirit, saints or prophets, who have had their hours of mediumship in which they have shown, sometimes in many forms, this faculty latent in their souls.

Neither high intelligence nor elevation of soul is inhibitory to such manifestations. If there are many mediumistic phenomena the form or the outcome of which leaves much to be desired, it is because high intelligence and great character are rare. These qualities found themselves united in Jeanne d'Arc, and that is why her psychic faculties attained so high a degree of power. One may say of the Maid of Orleans that she realized the complete ideal of mediumship.

∼

But now a question suggests itself. It is one of the highest importance. Who were these invisible personalities who inspired and directed Jeanne? Whence came these saints, these angels, these archangels? What are we to think of this constant intervention of Saint Michael, Saint Catherine and Saint Margaret? To solve this problem one must closely analyse the psychology of clairvoyants and of sensitives and understand that they must correlate the manifestations which come to them with the forms, names and appearances with which their education has familiarized them, and with the influences, beliefs, places and times wherein they lived. Jeanne d'Arc was no exception to this law. In order to describe her psychic perceptions she used the ideas, expressions and images which were familiar to her. That is what mediums of all ages have done. According to their own surroundings they give to the inhabitants of the occult world the names of gods, of genii, of angels, of demons or of spirits.

The invisible intelligences, when they intervene in human life, find that they too are obliged to conform to the mentality of those with whom they are in contact, and to use the forms and names of those illustrious beings who may be familiar to them with the object of exalting them, inspiring confidence, and preparing them the better for the part which is ordained.

Speaking generally, they do not in the Beyond attach so much importance to names and to personalities as we do. They are fulfilling high aims, and in order to realize them they make use of such means as the state of the human spirit, or as the level of inferiority and of ignorance in that particular place and time, seems to demand.

One might possibly offer the objection that these super-human powers could easily have revealed to the Maid of Domrémy their true character, initiating her into the higher and brighter knowledge of the invisible world and its law. But apart from the fact that it is a very long and difficult process to initiate even the most capable of human beings into those laws of higher life, which none of us even now thoroughly grasp, it would have been directly adverse to the object which was in view. It is clear that it would have hindered the work in hand, a work depending entirely on action, if one were to create in the heroine a state of mind and a view of her position which would have put her into opposition with that social and religious order under which she was called to act.

If one examines with attention what Jeanne reported of her Voices one is struck by one significant fact: it is that the spirit to which she gave the name of Saint Michael never once called himself by that name.

The two other beings were described by St. Michael himself under the name of St. Catherine and St. Margaret. We have to recollect that the statues of these saints adorned the Church of Domrémy where Jeanne used to go to pray every day. In her long meditations and her ecstasies she had continually in front of her eyes the images of these virgin martyrs.

On the other hand, the existence of these two people is more than doubtful. What we know of them is contained in legends. About the year 1600 one of the examiners of the University, Edmond Richer, who believed in angels, but not in St. Catherine nor in St. Margaret, broached the idea that these apparitions seen by the young girl were given to her under the outward semblance of saints whom she had venerated since her childhood. "The spirit of God which governs the Church accommodates itself to our infirmities," said he.

Later, another doctor at the Sorbonne, Jean de Launoy, wrote, "The life of St. Catherine, virgin and martyr, is entirely fabulous from beginning to end." We need only add one other witness. Bousuet, in his "History of France", drawn up for the instruction of the Dauphin, does not mention either these saints. In our own time, M. Marius Sapet, student of the School of Archives and member of the Institute, in his preface written for "The Life of St. Catherine" by Jean Mielot, is very cautious on the subject of the documents which were used in writing this word.

"The Life of St. Catherine," said he, "under the form which it takes in Manuscript 6449 in the National Library, has really no pretensions to canonical value."

We may remark that the more recent case of the Curé d'Ars presents many analogies to that of Jeanne d'Arc. Like her, this celebrated miracle worker was exalted and in touch with spirits, above all with Sr. Philomène, his habitual guardian angel. He also was subjected to persecution from a lower spirit named Grappin. Now, as in the case of Catherine and Margaret, Philomène does not represent a living being, but is merely a symbolic name. It means one who loves humanity.

If the names given to the invisible powers who influenced the life of Jeanne d'Arc have only a relative importance and are in themselves very doubtful, it is quite otherwise, as we have seen, with the objective reality of these powers and the constant effect which they produced upon the heroine.

Since the Catholic explanations seem insufficient, we are compelled to see in those powers superior beings who concentrate and put into action Divine forces at those moments when evil lies heavy upon the world, and when men by their actions retard or threaten the development of the eternal plan.

One finds these powers under the most varied names at different epochs of the world's history. But whatever name we give them their intervention in the affairs of men cannot be doubted. In the fifteenth century we see in them the protecting genius of France, the great spirits who particularly watch over the fate of our nation.

One may say that this is supernatural. No! What we really mean is that these are the elevated regions, the sublime heights, and if we may so express it, the background of all Nature.

By the inspiration of seers and prophets, by intermediary powers and by spirit messengers, humanity has always been in touch with the higher planes of the universe. The experimental studies of the last half century have thrown a certain light on the life of the Beyond. We know that the world of spirits is peopled by innumerable beings who occupy every stage in the ladder of evolution. Death does not change us from the point of view of morality. We find ourselves in space with all the qualities which we have acquired, but also with all our weaknesses and our faults. It follows from this that the terrestrial atmosphere is vibrant with souls in a low state of development, eager to manifest themselves to human beings, and it is this which sometimes makes communication dangerous and exacts a laborious preparation and plenty of common sense on the part of the experimenters. These studies show also that there are above us legions of benevolent and protecting souls, the souls of men who in their lives have suffered for good, truth and justice. They hover above poor humanity endeavouring to guide it along the straight road of its destiny. Far above the narrow horizons of earth, a whole hierarchy of invisible beings stretches up into the firmament. It is the Jacob's Ladder of the story, the ladder of higher intelligence and higher conscience which is graduated, and rises up to those radiant and powerful spirits who are the agents of the Divine forces. These invisible beings, as we have said, interfere sometimes in the life of people, but not always in so brilliant and obvious a manner as in the case of Jeanne d'Arc. More frequently their action is indirect and obscure, partly to preserve human free will, and still more because although these powers wish to be recognized, they wish also that man should have to make a personal effort and so educate himself for their recognition.

These great facts of history can only be compared to those patches of light which may be seen from time to time between drifting clouds and give us a glimpse of the profound and infinite firmament beyond. These cloud openings suddenly close once more because man is not yet ripe for the comprehension of the mysteries of the higher life.

As to the choice of forms and of means which these great beings employ when they intervene in our world affairs, we must recognize that our intelligence is too weak adequately to appreciate and judge them. Our faculties are powerless to measure the vast sweep of the plans of these invisible directors. But we know that the facts are incontestable and undeniable. At various times in the midst of the darkness which surrounds us, and the ebb and flow of events, in critical hours when a nation is in danger, or when humanity is wandering in the mist, suddenly a herald of the Supreme Power descends among us to remind mankind that infinite resources exist above them, and that they can draw upon these by their thoughts and prayers, so as to attract the help of those spirits whom some day by their merits and their efforts they may hope to join.

The intervention in human affairs of these high beings whom we may call the anonymous workers of the universe depends on a profound law which we shall now define more closely in order to make it more clear.

As a rule, as we have said, those higher beings who manifest to mankind, do not give themselves names, or if they do, they adopt symbolical names which describe their nature or the type of mission which has been assigned to them.

Why, then, since man here below is so eager to claim his deserts and so anxious to link his name with any ephemeral work, why, I repeat, is it that the great missioners of the Beyond, the glorious messengers from the Invisible, prefer to remain anonymous, or to take allegorical names? It is because the laws of our terrestrial world and those of the superior world, in which these spirits of redemption have their life, differ greatly from each other.

Down here personality is everything. The tyrannical ego predominates. It is the sign of our inferiority, the unconscious proof of our selfishness. Our present condition being so limited, it is logical that all our acts centre upon our own personality. We are always referred to that ego which means the identity of the being in its inferior stage of evolution amid the fluctuations of space and the changes of time.

In the higher spiritual spheres it is quite different. Evolution there follows more ethereal lines—lines which at a certain height mean combination, association, and what we can only describe as a co-operative unity of being.

The higher a member mounts and progresses in the infinite hierarchy, the more the angles of his personality disappear, while his individuality spreads out and widens in the universal life under the law of harmony and love.

The identity of the being of course remains, but his actions co-operate more and more in the general activity, that is to say, in the divine plan which that general activity represents.

It is in this that the infinite progress of a personal life consists —to approach continually nearer to the absolute Being without ever reaching Him, and to conform our own work more and more fully with the

Divine. When it has reached this height the spirit no longer calls itself by this or that name. It is no longer an individual, a limited personality, but rather one of the forms of infinite activity. It may be called legion. It belongs to a hierarchy of forces and of glories just as a spark of flame belongs to the activity of that furnace which gives it birth and nourishes it. There is an immense association of spirits all harmonized together by the laws of a glorious affinity, of an intellectual and moral sympathy and by the love which unites them, a sublime brotherhood, of which the ties of our earth are but a pale and fleeting reflexion.

Sometimes from these harmonious groups, from these dazzling Pleiades, a living ray detaches itself, a radiant form approaches, like a projection of celestial light to explore and to illuminate the shades of our dark world, to help in the raising of souls, to strengthen someone at the hour of a great sacrifice, to hold the head of a Christ in agony, to save a people, or to rescue a nation which is on the point of perishing. Such are the sublime missions which these messengers of the Beyond come to fulfill.

There is a law of solidarity in the Universe by which the higher spirits draw upwards towards themselves the younger or less developed entities. Thus a great magnetic chain connects the whole immensity of the cosmos, and binds all souls and all worlds into a single unity.

And as the sublimity of moral grandeur consists in doing good for good's sake, without any selfish reward for oneself, the ministering angels work under the double veil of silence and of anonymity, so that the glory and merit of their actions may have God alone as their source and as their end.

Thus the visions and voices of Jeanne may be explained, and the appearances of an archangel and of saints who have never existed as individuals with such earth names, but who are none the less living realities, radiant beings sent forth from divine sources. It is they who made Jeanne the liberator of her country.

Michel-Micael, the Strength of God. Margheritte-Margarita, the precious pearl. Catherine-Katarina, the pure virgin. All are symbolic names which reflect moral beauty and high power, and represent a radiation from the divine centre.

14

ANALOGOUS POWERS, ANCIENT AND MODERN

JEANNE D'ARC was then an intermediary between the two worlds—a powerful medium. For this she was burned at the stake. Such is, as a rule, the lot of messengers from on high. They are subjected to persecutions at the hands of men who neither wish to, nor can, understand them. The examples which they present and the truths which they speak are a reproach to terrestrial interests and a condemnation of the passions and errors of humanity.

It is the same in our days, although these are less barbarous than the Middle Ages which sent such people wholesale to the scaffold. Our age still persecutes the agents of the Beyond. They are neglected, treated with contempt and vilified. I speak of true mediums and not of the fraudulent ones who are admittedly numerous. These latter prostitute one of the grandest things in the world and by that they take upon themselves heavy responsibility in the future, for everything has to be paid for sooner or later. All our actions, good or bad, come back to us with their consequences. That is the law of destiny.

The manifestations of the invisible world are, as we have said, continually with us, but they differ much in degree. Deception and fraud are mixed sometimes with true inspiration. Beside Jeanne d'Arc you will find Catherine de la Rochelle and William the Shepherd, a brace of imposters. There are also true mediums who overtax their powers and act sometimes under the impulse of auto-suggestion. The source is not always pure. Sometimes the vision is dim, but there do occur phenomena so striking that in their presence doubt ceases to exist, and of such were the mediumistic facts which adorned the life of Jeanne d'Arc.

There is in mediumship, as in all things, infinite diversity, a graduation of power, and a sort of hierarchy. Almost all great men with a destiny, prophets, founders of religion, messengers of truth, and all who have proclaimed those higher principles by which human thought is elevated, have been mediums, for their lives have been in constant touch with the higher spiritual spheres.

I have shown elsewhere, founding my views on numerous and detailed cases, that genius may often be considered as one of the manifestations of mediumship. Men of genius are usually inspired in the highest sense of the word. Their works are like fires which God lights in the night of the centuries to illuminate the march of humanity. Since the publication of my book I have received numerous documents in support of this thesis. Later on I may quote some of them.

The whole philosophy of history may be summed up in these few words, the communion of the visible and of the invisible. It all emanates from high inspiration. The men of genius, the great poets, the learned men, the artists, the celebrated inventors, all are agents for the divine plan in this world, that majestic plan of evolution which slowly moves the soul upwards.

Sometimes those noble intelligences which watch over this evolution materialize themselves in order to render their influence more direct and efficacious. Thus you have Zoroaster, Buddha, and above all, the Christ. Sometimes they inspire and help the missionaries who have been sent down to give a stronger impulse to the springs of human thought. Moses, St. Paul, Mahomet and Luther were among these. But in every case human liberty is respected. Hence the obstacles of various sorts which these great spirits meet in their endeavour.

The most striking fact among the various signs which indicate the coming of these messengers from on high, is the insistence upon the religious idea on which such comings are based.

This idea is sufficient to exalt their courage and to rally round them, even though they are usually of humble birth and devoid of material forces, innumerable allies who are ready to adopt their thoughts, the grandeur of which has impressed itself upon their minds.

They have all spoken of their communication with the Invisible. All have had visions, heard voices, and recognized themselves as being the simple instruments of Providence for carrying out a mission. Alone, left to their own devices, they would not have succeeded. The higher influence was necessary and indispensable to the triumph of their ideas against which so many enemies raged.

Philosophy also has had its glorious inspired figures.

Socrates, like Jeanne d'Arc, was conscious of the

voices, or rather of one voice—that of a familiar spirit which he called his "daimon."

It could be heard at any time.

One may read in Plato how Timarchus would have avoided death if he had only listened to the voice of this spirit. "Do not go," said Socrates to him when he was leaving after his banquet with Philemon, his confederate, the only one who knew of his intention to kill Nicias. "Do not go, the voice tells me to restrain you." Although twice warned Timarchus did go, but failed in his enterprise, and was condemned to death. At the hour of his punishment he understood too late that he should have obeyed the voice.

"O, Clitomarchus," said he to his brother, "I am dying because I refused to act as Socrates advised me."

One day the voice warned the sage not to go further along the road on which he and his friends were walking. They refused to listen to it. They continued their journey and met a drove of stampeded horses who put their lives in danger.

After having experienced so often the wisdom of the advice given by him by this voice, Socrates had every reason to believe in it. He reminded his friends that, having told them the predictions which he had received, they had never once been able to show that he was mistaken.

Let us recall the solemn declaration made by this philosopher before the tribunal of the Ephetes, when it was for him a question of life or death.

"This prophetic voice of the daimon, which has never been silent during the whole course of my life, and which has never failed even under the most difficult circumstances, to turn me away from whatever might harm me – this divine voice, I say, is now silent whilst these misfortunes have overwhelmed me. Why is it? It is probably that what is happening to me is good for me. We deceive ourselves in supposing that death is a misfortune."

In France also our philosophers have been touched by the spirit. Pascal had hours of ecstasy. Recherche de la Vérité, by Malebranche, was written in the darkness, and Descartes tells us how sudden intuition as swift as lightning gave him the idea of his Doute Méthodique, a philosophic system in which we find all the germs of modern thought. In his "Medico Psychic Annals," Brierre de Boismont tells us:

"Descartes, after a long period of rest, was followed by an invisible entity, who persuaded him to continue his search for truth."

Schopenhauer in Germany was also conscious of being influenced from the Beyond.

"My philosophical postulates," said he, "have been developed in me apart from myself, at times when my will seemed to be paralysed, and my individuality to have no connection with the work."

Almost all the famous poets have enjoyed similar invisible help. Amidst them we may quote Dante and Tasso, Schiller and Goethe, Pope, Shakespeare, Shelley, Le Camoens, Victor Hugo, Lamartine, Alfred de Musset and others.

Many painters and musicians, Raphael, Mozart, Beethoven and others have had the same experience, for inspiration is for ever flowing in long silent waves down to humanity.

One may say that these ideas are in the air. So they are in truth, because it is the souls who are free in space who suggest them to mankind. Here one may search for the source of great movements of thought in every country. Here also lies the cause of those revolutions which destroy a country in order to rejuvenate it.

One must recognise, then, that the phenomenon of mediumship fills the whole of history. All our records become illuminated in this light. Sometimes it concentrates itself on one eminent personality and shines with a vivid luster, as in the case of Jeanne d'Arc. Sometimes it is diffused and spread over a great number of interpreters, as in our own days.

Mediumship has ever been the inspirer of genius, the educator of humanity, and the means which God employs to elevate and to change society. In the fifteenth century it served to draw France out of the abyss of trouble in which she was plunged. To-day it is like a fresh breeze which passes over the world, and brings renewed life to many souls stupefied by materialism, and to many truths thrust into the shade of oblivion.

The phenomena of clairvoyance, clairaudience, the visions of the dead, the manifestations of invisible life through materialization, automatic writing, raps, etc., are innumerable. Every day they increase amongst us.

The enquiries of many learned societies, the experience and the records of eminent savants, and of famous public men some of whose names we have given, leave no doubt at all as to the reality of the facts. They have been observed under conditions which put cheating out of the question. We will quote only a few of the more recent which present analogies to the life of Jeanne d'Arc.

First of all, let us take the Voices.

In "Human Personality," F. Meyers tells us of the voices heard by a friend under circumstances of danger.

François Coppée tells in the same way of a mysterious voice which called him by his name at certain critical moments of his life, so that even when asleep he has been awakened by its intervention.

"Assuredly I was not dreaming at that moment," says he, "and the proof is that in spite of the great emotion and the heart palpitations which I felt, I have always instantly replied, 'Who is there? Who is it that is speaking to me?'" But never has the voice replied to his appeal.

In the month of May, 1897, Mr. Wiltshire was awakened in the early morning by the sound of his own name pronounced by an invisible presence. As the voice insisted and gave him the impression of immediate and threatening danger, he ended by rising and going out. He arrived just in time to save the life of a young girl who was about to drown herself.

In "La Revue Scientifique et Morale du Spiritisme," Dr. Breton, a naval surgeon, President of the Society of Psychic Studies at Nice, reports the following fact:

"Mdlle. Lolla, a young Russian girl, being in the country house of her family in Russia, dreamed that she saw her mother enter her room, and say to her, 'Lolla, do not be afraid, but the barn is on fire.' On the following night, Mdlle. Lolla was suddenly awakened by her mother, who, coming into her room, cried, 'Lolla, do not be afraid, the barn is on fire,' the very words which she had heard in her dream. Mdlle. Lolla married. She wedded M. de R., a Russian officer. Her father-in-law died. Some time afterwards, young Madame de R. accompanied her mother-in-law to the family burial ground in order to pray over the tomb of the deceased. While kneeling and praying she heard distinctly a voice, which said to her: 'You also will be a widow, but you will not have the consolation of coming to pray over the tomb of my son.'

"The young woman hearing this voice fainted. Her mother-in-law came to her help, and when the girl revived, she explained the reason of her emotion.

"The Russo-Japanese War broke out. Colonel de R. received the order to go to the front. He died in Manchuria. His body, in its coffin, was transported with others to Mukden before being sent to Russia, but the troops who escorted it had to leave it behind during the retreat of the Russian Army. In spite of many enquiries they were never able to find out what became of this body.

"The prophecy, then, of the spirit of the father of Colonel de R. came true. The young widow never was able to pray over the tomb of her husband."

In all these cases, then, we have voices with prophetic powers, exactly as with Jeanne.

Let us now discuss the question of apparitions. Such cases are not rare in our days, and occasionally have been confirmed by means of photography.

La Revue of 15th January, 1909, contains a record from Mr. W. T. Stead which relates a fact of this nature. The great English journalist was as famous for his truthfulness as for his unselfish courage. On a matter of principle he was ready to oppose the whole of England. One remembers how, at the risk of his own personal interests and taking no account of the millions which he might inherit from Cecil Rhodes, he dared to state publicly that the latter was one of those who was responsible for the South Africa war. He even went so far as to demand that he should be punished by hard labour.

In the course of this same war Stead called upon a psychic photographer, in order to see if he could get some results, for the study of the occult world attracted him strongly. This photographer saw a figure enter the room in the company of Stead, which figure he had already observed some days before in his studio. It was agreed that he should try to photograph it, together with Stead. Whilst the photograph was being taken the figure, which was invisible to human eyes, said clairaudiently that his name was Piet Botha. Among the Bothas known to Stead there was none who had this particular name. On the photograph there came out, standing by his side, the clearly defined and characteristic figure of a Boer.

When peace was declared, General Botha came to London. Stead showed him the photograph. Next day he had a call from one of the South African delegates, Monsieur Wessel. He was much interested, and said to Stead:

"This man never knew you, for he never put foot in England. He is one of my relations. I have his portrait at my house."

"Is he dead?" asked Stead.

"He was the first Boer Commander killed at the siege of Kimberley," replied his companion. "His name was Petrus Botha, but we called him Piet for short."

On being shown the photograph the other delegates from the Boer States recognized the Boer soldier.

Sometimes (and it is one of the strongest arguments in favour of their truth) visions appear to young children who are incapable of scheming or fraud.

The Annals of Psychic Science, February 16th, 1901, quote many such facts. In one case it was a little girl two-and-a-half years old, who saw in different places and under different circumstances her own little sister, who had died some time before, and who was stretching out her hands to her.

In another case a child of three perceived, at the moment of her little brother's death, one of her dead aunts, and ran towards her, following her about the room.

Again, one reads in Brierre de Boismont (Medico-Psychological Annals, 1851):

"A young man of eighteen, of a steady, normal type, lived for the sake of his health at Ramsgate. In a walk to one of the neighbouring villages he entered a church at nightfall, and was struck with terror to see a vision of his mother, who had died some months before of a lingering and painful illness, which had excited pity from all around her. This figure formed itself between him and the wall and remained for a considerable time motionless. He got back to his lodgings dazed with terror. The same apparition having appeared in his own room for several consecutive nights, he fell ill and traveled over to Paris where his father lived. He resolved not to speak to the father of the matter for fear of adding to the grief which the loss of a beloved wife had already brought upon him.

He was obliged to sleep in the room of his father, and was surprised to find a light burning there all night. This was contrary to his father's usual habit. After several hours of insomnia caused by the glare of this light the son got out of bed and extinguished it. The father immediately rose in great agitation, and ordered him to light it again, which he did, very much astonished at the emotion of his father and at the signs of terror visible on his face.

Having asked him what the reason was for his trouble, he only received a vague reply, and a promise that some day he should be told.

A week after this event the young man, being unable to sleep on account of the constant light, tried for the second time to extinguished it, but the father sprang instantly from his bed, reproved him for his disobedience, and lit the lamp once more. He admitted to him then that every time he was left in darkness the phantom of his wife appeared before him, and remained immovable, standing there until the light was again renewed.

This story made a strong impression upon the mind of the young man, and fearing to increase his father's trouble by telling him his own adventure at Ramsgate, he left Paris and went to a town in the interior of France sixty miles away, to see his brother, who was lodging there, and whom he had not told what had happened to him for fear of ridicule.

He had hardly entered the house and exchanged the usual salutations when the son of the lodging-house keeper said to him: 'Has your brother ever shown any sign of lunacy? He came down last night in his shirt, declaring that he had seen the spirit of his mother, and that he dared not go back into his room. Then he actually fainted from fear.'"

One might add many facts of the same sort, all showing visions analogous to those of Jeanne. The dwellers in space neglect no means of manifesting themselves and of proving to us the reality of survival. The great spirits show a marked predilection for the phenomenon of possession, for it allows them to reveal themselves more completely and to display the range of their intellectual power. The medium plunged into sleep by an invisible magnetic power gives up his body for some short period to the spirits who take possession of it, and so get into touch with us by voice, gesture and bearing.

Sometimes their language is so suggestive and so imposing that one cannot have the slightest doubt as to their character, their nature, and their identity. If it is easy to imitate psychic phenomena, such as tilting tables, automatic writing, or visions of phantoms, the same cannot be said of facts which belong to the higher intellectual order. One cannot imitate talent and, still less, genius. I have often been the witness of such scenes, and they have left each time a profound impression. To live, if it be but for a moment, on intimate terms with great beings, is one of the rarest joys that one may have upon earth. It is by this gift of possession that I myself have been able to communicate with spirit guides and with Jeanne herself, and to receive from her the details and revelations some of which I have been able to incorporate in this work.

At the same time, if this faculty is a source of joy to the experimenter, it gives very little satisfaction to the medium himself, for he does not preserve, after awakening, any remembrance of what has passed during his absence from his body.

Mediumship exists in a latent condition among very many people. Everywhere around us, among young women and young men, these subtle faculties lie which may develop into ties between the human brain and the intelligences of space. What is wanted now are schools and methods by which these factors may be developed scientifically and systematically, and so perfected. The present absence of methodical preparation and of patient study prevents us from drawing from these seeds all the fruits of truth and wisdom which they might give. Very often, for want of knowledge and of regular development, they dry up or produce only poisoned flowers. But little by little we see a new science building itself up and conveying to all a knowledge of the laws which rule the invisible universe. Soon we shall learn to cultivate these precious faculties, and to turn them into instruments for those great souls who carry the secrets of the Beyond.

Experimenters will give up their narrow views and their old scientific routine, and will endeavour to cultivate the powers of the spirit by elevated thought and by high motives so as to join the higher world with our inferior spheres. Then an illumination from above will come to aid their researches. They will learn that in the study of great philosophical problems moral cultivation and rectitude of life are essential conditions of success.

If science and method are indispensable in the case of psychic experiment, a receptive attitude of soul by means of prayer is not less important, for it constitutes that loving current which draws down to us benevolent powers and repels evil influences. The whole life of Jeanne demonstrates this.

On the day when all these conditions are observed, the new psychic knowledge will enter fully into its own. At a time when so many beliefs are wavering and when the human soul is sunk in materialism, in the midst of the general weakening of character and of conscience, it will become a living and active faith which will re-unite Heaven to Earth and draw together souls and worlds in one eternal and infinite communion.

In the French original there follow after the biographical chapters several remarkable essays upon Jeanne d'Arc, which deal respectively with Jeanne and the idea of fatherland, Jeanne and the idea of religion, Jeanne and the Celtic spirit, the portraits of Jeanne, the military genius of Jeanne, the relation of Jeanne to the twentieth century, and finally Jeanne as she bears upon that modern psychic movement of which Monsieur Denis is persuaded that she is the standard-bearer. For the other essays the reader may be referred to the original, but this last one is of so extraordinary noble and elevated a character, and forms so beautiful a piece of prose imagery, that the translator hopes that even in his English version some reflexion of its beauty may be obtained, and that the reader, whatever his view upon psychic matters, will be glad to have it placed before him. As to the direct communications, each will form his own opinion, but there can be no two opinions as to the high aims of the writer, or the beauty of his message.

15

JOAN OF ARC AND THE MODERN PSYCHIC MOVEMENT

THE early days of Christianity were full of visions, apparitions, voices, premonitory dreams and other evidences of psychic power. The faithful drew from such things an overwhelming moral force which gave them strength to face every danger and torment. Since the most remote ages the invisible world has always communicated with our own, and a current of spiritual life has continually been guided down to our terrestrial humanity by prophets and mediums. It is this vital influx from supernatural sources, which has been the spring of every religion. All have in their origin shared this deep essential inspiration. So long as they preserved it pure, they kept their freshness and their vitality, but they faded away and died in exact proportion to the degree of separation which came between them and these secret sources of strength.

That is what has happened to orthodoxy. It has misunderstood or forgotten the great flood of spiritual power which bathed the Christian cult in its early days. It has burned by the thousand the agents of the unseen, rejected their teachings and silenced their voices. The trials for sorcery and the executions of the Inquisition have raised a barrier between the two worlds, and have stopped for centuries that spirit communion which, far from being an accidental thing, is really one of the fundamental laws of Nature.

The disastrous results may be traced all round us. Religions are now only the dried-up branches of a sapless trunk, because the roots are no longer in touch with the vital nourishment. They still tell us of the survival of the individual and of the future life, but they are unable to furnish the least actual proof of it. So is it also with all systems of philosophy. If faith has weakened and if materialism and atheism have rapidly increased, if crime and animal passion and suicide are all so prevalent, it is because the upper life no longer descends to fertilize human thought, and because the idea of immortality is no longer reinforced by actual demonstration. The development of scientific thought and of the critical spirit has made mankind more and more exacting. Mere assertions will no longer content him. He asks for facts and proofs.

Consider for a moment how overwhelmingly important it would be could we formulate a science, a revelation, based upon a solid groundwork of phenomenal experience, which would afford us a definite proof of survival, and at the same time demonstrate that justice is not a vain phrase – and that each of us finds in the Beyond an environment which shall be in exact proportion to our own deserts.

This is precisely what modern Psychic Religion does offer. It contains within it the seeds of a mental revolution which shall embrace ideas, faiths, opinions and ethics. Hence the urgent necessity to study these facts, to classify them, to analyze them with care, and to note the deductions which may be drawn from them.

The moral state of Society has become gravely disquieting. In spite of the spread of education crime increases. Theft, murder and suicide do not become less common. Morals are corrupt. Discontent and disillusionment sink ever deeper into the heart of man. The horizon is dark, and far off on hears the low mutterings which seem to be threats of a social storm. In nearly every class of society journalism has degraded the character and the conscience. Ideals seem to have faded out of the souls of the people. They say: "Eat, drink, grow richer—all the rest is a mere shadow." There is no God but money, no object in life but pleasure. Passions, greed, appetites are unrestrained. This flood of evil mounts up like a rising wave and threatens to submerge the world.

Still, there are many noble souls who ponder over it and who grieve. They feel that matter is not all. There are times when humanity mourns for the lost ideal and feels the emptiness and the instability of worldly things. It is borne in upon them that what they are taught is insufficient, that life is broader, the world more vast, and the Universe more marvelous than is supposed. Man searches, experiments, and asks. He wants not merely an ideal, but rather some certainty which may sustain and console him amid the trials and sufferings of life. He asks himself what is to be the final outcome of this transitional age, which has seen the death of so many systems and traditions, the dust of which now lies around us.

By its obstinacy in shutting itself up in the narrow circle of dogma, and by its refusal to enlarge its conception of human destiny and of the Universe, orthodox religion has estranged the picked brains of humanity, and the majority of those whose opinion has real weight in the world. The public has followed the intellectuals. The eyes of humanity are turned towards science. They have long asked from it some solution of the problem of existence. But science up to now, in spite of its magnificent conquests, has been too deeply imbued with material theories to furnish man with a notion of his position and of the destiny which would exalt him, giving him fresh strength and inspiration.

Thus it was that the invisible world, that world which the Church has opposed, though shrouded in the shadow for centuries, came afresh into action. It is now showing its presence in every part of the globe, under many forms, and by the most varied means. It has come to show man the sure and the straight way which will lead him to the heights.

Everywhere psychic faculties are disclosing themselves, inexplicable phenomena are appearing. Societies for the study of them, and journals to report them are coming into existence, each of them a centre of light from which these new ideas radiate out into a darkened world. These Spiritual Societies are already numerous enough to make a chain round our planet. Through them, for the last fifty years, there has been preparing and germinating those seeds which grow in obscurity but are destined to be the flowers of the coming age. This is what we call Modern Spiritualism, not a religion in the narrow sense of the word, but rather a science, a crown of all human work and thought, a revelation which will draw mankind out of the maze in which it has wandered, enlarge its horizon, and draw it up to participate in the life of the great spaces—the infinite, the universal life.

The modern psychic movement means the study of man, not in his transitory corporal form, but in his spirit, in his imperishable reality and in his evolution through the ages. It is the study of transcendental thought and of the inner consciousness. It deals with the questions of responsibility and duty, and with all the problems of life and death viewed from the invisible world as well as from here. It means the application of these problems to moral progress, the common good and social harmony.

Material life is a passing thing. Our existence is but an instant, a dot amid an immensity. Man is a thinking and self-conscious atom upon the globe which sustains him, and this globe is itself only an atom moving in a boundless Universe. But our future is as infinite as that Universe, and the worlds which gleam our heads at night are part of our heritage.

The modern psychic knowledge teaches us to come out from the narrow circle of our daily work, and to be in touch with that vast field of activity which is open to us. The great enigma becomes more simple and the divine plan unrolls itself before us. Nature takes on a meaning. It becomes the wonderful ladder of evolution, the stage on which the soul endeavours to shake off matter and to mount from the lower, darker life towards the light.

A common harmony unites all those who are on the varied rungs of this ladder, or on all the different planes of life. Man is no longer alone when he strives and suffers in the cause of truth and of good. An invisible company assist and inspire him, as they did Jeanne d'Arc and her brave companions.

This harmony of the Universe is especially noticeable at the present epoch. In hours of crisis when souls weaken and when humanity stumbles upon its difficult road, the invisible world intervenes. Celestial spirits, the messengers of space, work with us. They direct the sequence of events and stimulate our minds. Above all they strive to re-establish those broken bonds which should unite the two worlds. They say so themselves in these terms:

"Listen to our voices, you who strive and weep. You have not been abandoned. We have striven to establish communication between your forgetful world and this world of ours which does not forget. We have devised a tie which is still weak, but which will become strong. It is mediumship. Soon it will no longer be despised and persecuted. Men will no longer be able to ignore it. It is the only possible intermediary between the living and the dead. Now that the door is open it will not be closed until troubled mankind has learned to struggle up from the darkness into the light of heaven." JOHN, Disciple of Paul.

It comes at the right time, this new revelation, and it assumes the character which the spirit of the times calls for—the scientific and philosophic spirit. It does not come to destroy but to build up. The aid of the spirit world will enable us to see into the depths of the past as well as of the future. It will raise from the dust of centuries forgotten beliefs, and will give them new life by completing and explaining them. To the dark words "one must die," words of fear and of threat, it will add the vital words "one must live again." Instead of the terrors inspired by the fears of hell, it gives us joy of the soul, bringing us into an immense, radiant and glorious life. To all the despairing people upon earth, to the weak, to the disappointed, it offers the chalice of strength filled with the generous wine of hope and immortality.

Let us return to Jeanne d'Arc. It may seem that the points discussed have carried us far from our subject. It is not really so. These considerations help us to understand better the missions of Jeanne. We say "missions," for her actual work, though less apparent, is quite as important now as it was in the fifteenth century. Let us discuss it.

What was Jeanne in reality when she appeared on the great stage of history? Jeanne was a celestial messenger and, to use the expression of Henri Martin, "a Messiah." How many do we define with such terms? Let us leave the task to the spirit people themselves. Here is what one of our guides says upon the point:

"When men have forgotten their duty, God sends a messenger to them as an aid, that they may fulfill their work here more easily and more earnestly. These are what we call Messiahs. At that sad hour when souls sink into materialism they demonstrate by their inspired voices the truth which calls out to mankind. Observe how they always come at moments of crisis, when everything spiritual seems to be in danger of eclipse from the fogs of self-interest and passion. They are like the evening breeze which comes to calm the tumultuous waves seething from the storms of the day. Ask, and divine aid will be given to you, even as our Master promised. But do not repulse the messenger. Learn to understand him. He is the ambassador of God and he is clothed with the light of His truth, so you owe him your respect.

People cannot always distinguish these higher beings or appreciate the loftiness of their souls. They picture Messiahs as being different from people of flesh and blood, and they do not recognize them when they appear. Thus it comes about that the messenger of the Lord usually ends his celestial mission by supreme personal sorrow. Read the records, and you will find that all those whom humanity has finally honoured have died unnoticed, or else have been betrayed and sacrificed. This is in order that their mission may also show the grandeur of suffering. The last word which you will find on the lips of the Master and of all great martyrs has been: 'Pardon them, for they are ignorant.'" JOHN, The Disciple of Paul.

Jeanne was one of these Messiahs sent to save people who were in agony, but for whom a great future was waiting. France was called to play a considerable part in the world. Her history has proved it. She had the necessary qualities for the task. One might fairly say that though some other nations might be more serious, more thoughtful and more practical, none possesses the heart-qualities and the adventurous generosity, which has made France the apostle and soldier of justice and liberty the whole world over. This predestined part could only be played by France if she were free, and yet her faults had brought her to within imminent danger of extinction. Until Jeanne appeared, all Europe believed that the mission of the great French nation, the origin of so much that was noble, was at an end. She above all others had been the origin of chivalry, had promoted the Crusades, and had founded the arts of the Middle Ages. She had been the first in civilization in the West. And yet all human power seemed to have been unable to save this glorious country. But that which man could not do, a high spirit with the invisible world behind her was able to accomplish.

Here a question arises. Why did God choose the hand of a woman to draw France from the tomb? Michelet has thought that it was because France is herself essentially feminine—a woman at heart. Or is it, as other writers have said, because woman is superior to man in certain sentiments —in pity, tenderness and enthusiasm? No doubt this is so, and there lies the secret of the devotion of woman and of her spirit of sacrifice.

In the fifteenth century, as Henri Martin has pointed out, all the energies of the stronger sex, the sex formed for the life of action, were exhausted. The last reserve of France lay in her women, with divine power to sustain them. That is why Heaven sent us her whom the voices called "The Daughter of God."

But there may be a higher reason. It may be that God, making mock of the weakness of the strong and the folly of the wise, chose to save France by the hand of one who was almost a child, in order that when they compared the weakness of the instrument with the grandeur of the result, mankind could no longer doubt that in this work of salvation they saw the action of a higher Power and the intervention of the Almighty.

One might then ask, if Jeanne was a messenger from Heaven, why so many vicissitudes and such difficulties in her work of deliverance? Why these hesitations, intrigues, set-backs and these treasons around her?

When Heaven intervenes and God sends His messengers upon earth, can there be impediments and resistance to their action?

We touch here the great problem. Above all one must realize this – that man is a free agent, and that all humanity has responsibility. There is no responsibility without liberty. Free humanity has to bear the fruits of its own actions from age to age. The same beings come back from age to age. The same beings come back from century to century to make history and to gather in their new life the sweet and bitter fruits of joy or of sorrow, which they have sown in their former lives. Forgetfulness of the past is only temporary, and proves nothing against the law. Humanity is free, but freedom without wisdom, without reason, without illumination, leads to the abyss. The blind man is free, and yet without a guide what is his freedom worth to him? This is the reason why humanity has always needed to be upheld, guided, protected, and in some degree inspired by Providence. But it is better that this support should not be too obvious, for if a higher Power openly took charge, then it would become a constraint. It would weaken and even annihilate freedom of action. Man would lose the merit due to his initiative. He would no longer rise by his own merits. The divine end would be frustrated. Hence the difficulty of direct intervention at every time of trouble. What, then, can the messenger from on high, the minister of the eternal will, do under these limitations? He cannot impose himself—he can only offer himself, so that the individual may remain free to determine his own fate.

This is the explanation of the mission of Jeanne, her triumphs and defeats, her glory and her martyrdom. It also explains the law which governs spiritual power when it acts upon humanity. The influence which God exerts upon the earth can only act to the extent that humanity receives it. If it is welcomed and obeyed, it becomes active and beneficent. If it is repulsed, it remains powerless. The messenger, the Messiah, loses his touch on earth.

Humanity is advancing through the centuries to conquer the supreme good things—truth, justice and love. These good things it must reach by its own efforts. It is the law of its destiny, the very reason for its existence. But in hours of trouble, of crisis and of reaction, Heaven sends down its missionaries to distracted, despairing mankind.

Jeanne was one of these. Like all the divine messengers she arose among the poor and humble. Her infancy has that in common with Christ. It is a law of history and a lesson from God that the greatest things come from below. Christ was the son of a poor carpenter. Jeanne was a peasant girl. These two Messiahs chose here neither knowledge nor wealth. What need had they for either? The children of this world have need of material power and of science to carry out their designs. Messiahs have only to accomplish what is preordained. They possess inherent force.

Jeanne had a double mission which she still carries out upon the spiritual side of life. To France she brought a revelation of the Invisible and of the forces which it holds. She brought knowledge and a message which will echo down the centuries.

This message was beyond the comprehension of the Middle Ages. To bring it to the full, four centuries of work and progress were needed. That is why the Supreme Will has so arranged it that for four hundred years the memory of Jeanne was obscured by shadows, and that now there is a glorious re-awakening. Today this figure reappears radiant from the obscurity of the ages. Human thought is ready now to understand this problem and to investigate this spirit world, the existence of which finds its strongest affirmation in the life and mission of Jeanne.

Jeanne had her guardians, her spirit guides, and it is well to note that on a lower scale the same may be said for each of us. Every human being has near him an invisible friend who helps, comforts, and directs him aright if he will but follow the direction. Often they are those who have loved us upon earth, a father, a vanished mother, a spouse who has passed on. Many beings watch over us, and try to guard us from the instincts and the passions which push us towards evil. Whether one calls them our familiar genii, as did the Greeks, or our guardian angels, as do the Catholics, is of little importance. The fact remains that we all have our guides, our secret sources of inspiration. All of us have our voices.

But while in the case of Jeanne these voices were exterior, objective and perceived by the senses, in our case they are usually internal, intuitive and sounding only in the region of our conscience.

Have you not yourself heard these voices, you who read this? They speak in the silence. They tell you what to work for, and how to raise yourselves in raising others. Surely you have all heard the voice which, within the sanctuary of your heart, calls you to duty and to sacrifice. When you hear it anew, rouse yourselves, elevate your thoughts. Ask and you shall receive. Call upon the divine forces. Search, study, meditate, that you may be initiated into the great mysteries. So by degrees you will find new powers stir within you. A light unknown to you before will descend in waves upon you, the sweet flower of hope will open within you and you will be filled with that force which gives you assurance of the invisible and confidence in divine Justice. Then all life will become easy to you. Your thoughts, instead of dragging sadly in the heavy atmosphere of terrestrial doubts and contradictions, will rise above them all, and will be enlightened and invigorated by inspiration from above.

One must remember that in each of us lies, useless and unproductive, an infinite treasure.

There may be apparent barrenness and sadness, sometimes even disgust of life. But open your heart, let the ray shine into it, and then a more intense and beautiful life will awaken within you. You will take pleasure in a thousand things to which you were indifferent and which will charm your days. You will feel yourself grow stronger, you will walk with a firmer step, and your soul will be as a temple filled with light, splendour, and harmony.

∼

Jeanne d'Arc, as we have said, was a messenger from the spirit world, one of God's mediums. She realizes in our history the higher ideal of mediumship. But none the less that which she possessed in so eminent a degree may become the heritage of many upon a more humble scale.

We have already quoted those prophetic words—"When the time has come I will spread my spirit over all flesh. Your young people will see visions and your old will dream dreams" (Acts ii. 17).

All seems to indicate that this time is now at hand. The prophecy is actually coming true, all around us. That which in the past was the privilege of a few is becoming more and more universal. Already, down in the heart of the people there are signs and portents which point to a new era. Before long all that makes for the beauty and grandeur of human genius, all the glories of civilization, will be renewed and nourished from this immense source of inspiration which will open to the spirit of a man a boundless field in which he may build up the past. All the arts—philosophy, letters, science, music, and poetry—will drink from these springs of inspiration, and will be transformed under the all-powerful breath of the infinite.

The mission of the new knowledge, like that of Jeanne, is a mission which is faced with terrible obstacles. It is marked by signs, portents, and all that can indicate divine sanction. Its tasks is to defeat the enemy, and that enemy today is the materialist, the pessimist, the cold and dark philosophy, which can only lead to the selfish search for enjoyment, or to despair.

But it has to walk its "via dolorosa." It is the lot of every new idea. At this moment the hour of its trial has come. Like Jeanne before her examiners at Poitiers, the new Revelation stands to be judged by the faiths and systems of the past, by the theologians and the representatives of a narrow conventional science. Against her are ranked all the authorities, all the champions of old and incomplete ideas, ideas which have become inadequate to the needs of mankind and which must yield to the new impulse which claims its place in the world.

At the present time this solemn trial is taking its course before an interested humanity, whose own future fate is involved in the verdict. What will that verdict be? Doubt is impossible to those who know the facts. How can one hesitate between the young growing idea and the stale systems which weaken with the years. Humanity must live, prosper, and increase, and it is not among ruins that it can find its abiding-place.

The new knowledge stands before the tribunal of public opinion. It addresses the churches and the powers of this world, and it says to them:

"You have in your hands all the means of action which secular authority can give you, and yet you can do nothing against materialism, crime and immorality, which spread like a foul ulcer. You are impotent to save humanity in its hour of danger. Do not remain deaf, then, to the appeals of this new spiritual force, for it brings you the power you need for the regeneration of

Society. Appeal to all that is great and beautiful in the soul of man and say to him:

'Raise yourself! Elevate your aspirations, O human soul! Advance with confidence towards your glorious future. The infinite powers will help you, nature will be your ally in the work, the stars in their courses will light your path.

'Advance, human soul, strong in the powers which lie behind you! Go, like Jeanne in her battles, to face the world of matter and the play of passions. At your call Society will change and ancient forms will dissolve to give place to new combinations, and younger organizations richer in light and in life.'"

As to Jeanne, her influence has persisted in the world after her leaving it. It is by that influence that France was delivered from the English, not in one single campaign, nor by a steady process like the rise of the tide, as might have been the case had all men had the same confidence and faith as she, but after many vicissitudes and alternations of failure and success. The soul of Jeanne, so full of love and of desire for good, could not remain quiescent in eternal beatitude. At the present moment she is returning to us with another mission, in order to do upon the spiritual and moral plane, over a larger field, that which she did for France upon the material plane. She sustains and inspires the acolytes of the new faith and all those who bear in their hearts an unconquerable confidence in the future.

Know, then, that a revolution greater than any ever known in the world has begun, a peaceful and regenerating revolution. It will tear human routine out of its age-long ruts and will raise the thoughts of man to the splendid destiny which awaits him.

The great souls of the past will reappear among us. Their voices will be heard again. They will exhort mankind to hasten its march. And the soul of Jeanne is one of the most powerful amid that band who work upon the world, preparing a new era for humanity. This is the reason why fresh light is given us at present upon the character of Jeanne and her mission. By her aid and that of the great spirits who are with her the hopes of those who aspire to good and seek for justice will be fulfilled.

The radiant band of these spirits whose names shine down the vistas of history, the great initiates of the past, the prophets of every nation, the messengers of truth, all are joined in the work. But above all is Jeanne, exhorting us to fresh effort. All cry to us:

"Up! Not for the clash of swords as of old, but for the struggles of the soul. Up! To resist an invasion more deadly than that of the foreigner, to hold off materialism, sensualism, the abuse of pleasure, the ruin of the ideal—everything, in fact, which depresses, enervates and enfeebles us. Up! To work and strive for intellectual safety and the regeneration of our race and of humanity."

This great soul floats above us. On many occasions she has been able to make herself audible and to say what she thought of the reasons which have brought her back to us, and the nature of the forces which have sustained her. Yielding to prayer she has consented to sum up all her thoughts in a message which we reproduce, as in duty bound, with scrupulous fidelity. It is the most worthy conclusion which can be given to this essay.

A MESSAGE

SWEET is the communion with those who love our Lord and Father even as I do. I am not saddened by the vision of the past, for it draws me to you, and my remembrance of my communion with the holy dead makes me the sister and the comrade of all those to whom God has granted the favour of knowing the secret of life and death.

I return thanks to God for permitting me to draw close to you, and to tell who know a little that the lives which God gives us must be used wisely if we are to be in His grace. All life should be sweet and welcome which enables us to do the task assigned to us by the All-powerful Father and Judge. We should bless all that comes from His hand.

He has always chosen the weak to carry out His plans, for He can give strength to the lamb, even as He promised. He brings truth under the most changing forms, but all cannot understand His purpose. Submissive to His laws and trying to follow them, I have not always understood them. I knew, however, that the sweet counsels which He gave me could not be the work of an enemy, and the comfort which they have always given me has been a stay in trouble and a heart's joy. I never knew what was the deeper design of the Lord. He hid from me in all His messages the dreadful end which I was to endure, having pity on my weakness and on my shrinking from pain, but when the time did come, He gave me strength and courage.

I love to think of the hours when first I heard the voices. I cannot say that I was afraid. I was greatly astonished to find myself the subject of the Divine Mercy. I knew instantly that they were the messengers of God, and I felt a great sweetness in my heart whilst the holy voice rang in my ears. It is not possible for me to tell you exactly how I felt, for I could not describe the deep peace and joy, so that when they ceased I felt that I was the child of God and of Heaven. I feebly comprehended that their will should be mine, but though overjoyed at their coming, I was surprised at the orders they gave and feared a little to execute them. It did certainly seem a fine work to save our France, but how was a girl to go among men-at-arms? Finally, in their sweet and constant companionship I came to have more confidence in myself, and the love which I had ever had for God guided my conduct, for it cannot be right to rebel against the will of a Father.

It was a hard task, and yet I had joy in obeying, and I set forth to do the Will of God. I am happy that I followed His orders, and I pardon those who were the instruments of my death, for I know that it was not out of hatred for my spirit that they set it free, but because they hated the work that I had done.

This work had been blessed by God, and, therefore, they were deeply in the wrong, but, like them, I have no hatred for their spirits. I am only the enemy of all that God condemns, or falseness and wickedness. It is their work which is evil. They return to it ever, but the remembrance of their past cannot be effaced by them. I mourn for the hatreds which they have encouraged among those who should be brothers, and for the evil weeds which they have sown in the Church, which have caused this Mother whom I once cherished to devote herself rather to theology than to charity. It is pleasing to me to see that they improve and admit to some extent their error, but things have never been as I should have wished them, and my love for the Church turns more and more away from this ancient guide of souls in order to give itself more completely to our sweet and gracious Lord."

JEHANNE.

TRANSLATOR'S NOTE

THE foregoing document has been difficult to reproduce, as it is in a French, which both in idiom and in construction is reminiscent of the Middle Ages. The sentences, too, are longer and more involved —sometimes more obscure—than the short, lucid style of Monsieur Denis.

From the point of view of an English Spiritualist, it is an interesting claim which Monsieur Denis makes, when he asserts that Jeanne d'Arc is one of the leaders upon the other side in bringing fresh religious truth to mankind.

Spiritualists have always held that the movement is an organized one, and that the same great spirits which were once notable upon earth are still leaders among their fellows, and busy in the glorious work of bringing fuller information to mortals. These leaders are often those who have actually played a part in the long fight from 1848 onwards, during which the new knowledge, amid much misrepresentation and persecution, has gradually spread.

These souls, whom we have known in life, can be more easily identified, but we have long been aware that behind them were other and greater powers who were using them as instruments. Monsieur Denis' thesis that among these is the beautiful and unselfish spirit of Jeanne d'Arc is a deeply interesting one.

It should be added that it has received some corroboration among our own mediums, and that the appearance of a maid in shining armour is one of the visions which has again and again been reported by our clairvoyants, who had heard nothing of the views of Monsieur Denis.

THE END

Copyright © 2021 by FV Éditions
Cover Design: Canva.com
Ebook ISBN : 979-10-299-1197-2
Paperback ISBN : 979-10-299-1198-9
Hardcover ISBN : 979-10-299-1199-6
All rights reserved.

www.ingramcontent.com/pod-product-compliance
Lightning Source LLC
LaVergne TN
LVHW041945070526
838199LV00051BA/2913